FRANCISCAN READINGS

Franciscan Readings, English Version of Vitam Alere, edited by Fr. Marion A. Habig OFM, Copyright © 1979 by Franciscan Herald Press, 1434 West 51st Street, Chicago, Illinois 60609. Reprint copyright ©1998 by Franciscan Herald Press, 1800 College Avenue, Quincy, Illinois, Quincy, Illinois 62301-2699. All rights reserved. Scripture readings used with permission from *The Bible – The Old Testament Vol. I* of Msgr. Ronald Knox, Copyright 1948, and *Volume II* in trans. of Msgr. Ronald Knox, Copyright 1950, Sheed & Ward, Inc., New York.

Library of Congress Cataloging in Publication Data:

Main entry under title:

Franciscan Readings

(Tau Series)
1. Franciscans – Prayer-books and devotions – English
2. Meditations   I. Habig, Marion Alphonse, 1901-
BX2188.F7V5713   242'.2   79-1127
ISBN 0-8199-0769-3

Nihil Obstat:
  Mark P. Hegener, OFM
  Censor Deputatus
Imprimatur:
  Msgr. Richard A. Rosemeyer, J.C.D.
  Vicar General, Archdiocese of Chicago
August 1, 1979

MADE IN THE UNITED STATES OF AMERICA

The "Tau" Series

The Tau was the talisman of St. Francis of Assisi. It takes its shape from Greek letter Tau (T), which is a cross. This method of forming the cross is very ancient, and goes back even to the days of the Old Testament. "Go through the midst of Jerusalem," spoke the Lord God to the destroying angel, "and mark Tau upon the foreheads of the men that sigh and mourn for all the abominations that are committed in the midst thereof." (Ezech. 9, 4). Historians generally admit that Francis was present at the Fourth Lateran Council, opened November 11, 1215 at St. John Lateran at which Pope Innocent III gave the opening address. After depicting the profanation of the Holy Places of the Saracens, the Pontiff deplored the scandals dishonoring Christ's flock, threatening it with God's punishments if it did not reform. He recalled Ezekiel's famous vision in which the Lord God, his patience exhausted, cries out in a loud voice: and after quoting the passage above, the Pope continued: "The TAU has exactly the same form as the Cross on which our Lord was crucified on Calvary. And only those will be marked with this sign and will obtain mercy, who have mortified their flesh and conformed their life to that of the Crucified Savior."

How could Francis, who saw God's hand in everything, be other than impressed by this proclamation which expressed so well his ideal of life and his dream of an apostolate. The fact is that the TAU, which the Pope made the emblem of the reform, became from then on Francis' own blazon, talisman and signature.

The TAU SERIES of books is to be published in this spirit. It will endeavor to indicate the extent and the direction of the great Franciscan movement in every field of life and culture. At the same time the series will be geared to interpret the man and the movement in the terms of modern life. For the publisher feels that the greatest danger to St. Francis' fame today is that he should lose reality and become little more than a popular figure in a saintly fairy land.

CONTENTS

FOREWORD

The nature and purpose of this book is explained in the Introduction by Fr. Angelo Orduña, editor of the original Latin work which is entitled *Vitam Alere*. Printed at the Portiuncula in Assisi, it was published "pro manuscripto" by the General Curia of the Order of Friars Minor, Rome, in 1977. This little paper-back book suggests a series of spiritual readings for a period of thirty-one days, three for each day. Two of the three, however, which are selections from Holy Scripture, are merely indicated by title, chapter, and verse. The third reading for each day is an excerpt from early Franciscan writings, the Latin texts being taken from Fr. K. Esser's recent new edition of the Writings of St. Francis, from *Analecta Franciscana*, and from other sources as mentioned in each case.

In our authorized English version the sixty-two Scriptural readings (two for each day) are printed out in full; and they are taken, with permission, from Monsignor Ronald Knox's translation of the Bible (Sheed and Ward). Most of the readings from the writings of St. Francis and other early Franciscan writings are taken from *St. Francis of Assisi: English*

Omnibus of Sources (3rd edn., 1977). Fr. August Rey-
ling of Quincy College made new translations from the
Latin, of the six readings taken from Fr. Hugh of
Digne's Exposition of the Franciscan Rule (edited by
A. Sisto, 1971), and of the reading from the Writings
of St. Clare (edited by I. Omaechevarria, 1970). He
also translated Fr. Orduña's Introduction. Fr. Hugh
of Digne was a Friar Minor of the thirteenth century,
born at Digne, France. Besides writing an Exposition
of the Rule, he was the author of other ascetical
treatises, notably *Tractatus de triplici via in sapien-
tiam perveniendi*. He died in Marseilles about 1285.

If this anthology and treasury of Franciscan
Readings is placed in the hands of every English-
speaking Friar Minor in the world and he uses it often, it cannot but make better Franciscans of all of us.
Though designed for the members of the Order of Friars Minor (O.F.M), it will undoubtedly be very help-
ful also to all other Franciscans, First and Second and
Third Orders, Regular and Secular.—Fr. M.A.H.

INTRODUCTION
By Fr. Angelus Orduña O.F.M.

As is universally known, the revision of the Calendar proper to the Order—in accordance with the Apostolic Letter "Mysterii Paschalis" and the Decree of the Sacred Congregation for Divine Worship, in which the rules for its execution were promulgated— brought about, especially in the Office of the Readings, a notable curtailment of those texts which contained the spirituality specifically Franciscan and promoted our Franciscan way of life.

It was immediately observed that to neglect or discard such a fruitful source of inspiration was entirely unbecoming. With this consideration in mind, the Minister General, the Very Reverend Father Constantine Koser, offered the proposal that from Franciscan authors those texts should be selected which excellently set forth the Franciscan type of spirituality. A collection of such texts, bound together in a single booklet and arranged as Readings throughout the space of about one month, could most appropriately be called "Franciscan Month."

The General Definitorium gave the proposal due consideration and then unanimously agreed that it would be suitable to draw up such a booklet of Readings specifically Franciscan; moreover, since a General Chapter was fast approaching, they decided to include in their "Report to the Chapter" a proposal to this effect, so that the members of the Chapter could express their opinion on this matter and then reach a final decision.

Accordingly, in the Chapter of Medellin, there was established a "Sixth Commission," charged with the task of "examining the Report concerning the actions and the plans bearing on the re-arrangement of the Roman-Seraphic Liturgy." This Commission drew up suitable resolutions to be submitted to the members of the Chapter for their consideration and their vote. In the sixth plenary session, on September 9, all the Voters—with one single exception—voted in favor of the booklet of Franciscan Readings to be used as an optional supplement.

After the Chapter, the task of selecting suitable texts was given to Father Cajetan Esser, to be assisted by Fathers D. Lapsanski, L. Falcon, A. Ghinato, and D. Kalverkamp. Father Hartdegen zealously worked at collecting the texts from Sacred Scripture. The work was successfully completed within a short time, but for various reasons it could not be published at that time.

But now, on the occasion of the 750th anniversary of the glorious death of our Father Saint Francis, the General Definitorium has judged it most useful to publish this booklet of Franciscan Readings.

These Readings may be used, according to their suitableness, either during the time of spiritual recollection or of Retreat, or on the occasion of Conventions of the Friars, or in the recitation of the Office as Readings as an alternate Reading according to the norm of arrangements in vogue, or for spiritual reading or meditation, either private or in common.

Here then is the story and the purpose of the booklet you have at hand, which represents a short summary of Franciscan spirituality.

As we cheerfully offer to all Friars this little work, we heartily implore that it may be for them instrumental in understanding the charism of our Father Saint Francis and an incentive to imitate the example of his life.

1

MY GOD AND MY ALL

READING I   Dt 6:4-25
A Reading from the Book of Deuteronomy

Listen then, Israel; there is no Lord but the Lord
our God, and thou shalt love the Lord thy God with
the love of thy whole heart, and thy whole soul, and
thy whole strength. The commands I give thee this
day must be written on thy heart, so that thou canst
teach them to thy sons, and keep them in mind continually, at home and on thy travels, sleeping and
waking; bound close to thy hand for a remembrancer,
ever moving up and down before thy eyes; the legend
thou dost inscribe on door and gate-post.

A time will come when the Lord has granted thee
entrance into the land which he promised to thy
fathers, Abraham, Isaac and Jacob; when he has
given thee possession of cities great and fair, not of
thy building, houses that abound in wealth, not of thy
making, wells not of thy digging, vineyards and
oliveyards not of thy planting; when thou hast eaten
of these and taken thy fill. Then beware; then thou
wilt be in danger of forgetting that it was the Lord
brought thee out of the land of Egypt, where thou
hadst dwelt in slavery. Thou shalt worship the Lord
thy God, to him only shalt thou do service, and swear

by no other name than this. All the neighbouring
peoples have their own gods; do not fall away into
worship of them; the Lord thy God, who dwells so
close to thee, is jealous in his divine love, and if he is
roused to anger with thee, he will sweep thee off the
face of the earth. Thou shalt not put the Lord thy God
to the proof, as thou didst at the Place of Challenge; it
is for thee to live by his commandments, by the decrees and observances he has enjoined on thee, to obey
the Lord's good pleasure. So shalt thou prosper, and
the fair land which the Lord promised to thy fathers
shall be thine to have and to hold; he will be true to
his word, and dispossess all those enemies of thine at
thy onslaught.

And so, in time to come, when one of thy sons asks
thee what is the meaning of all the decrees and observances and awards which the Lord your God has
given you, this shall be thy answer: We dwelt in
Egypt once, as Pharao's slaves, and the Lord our God
rescued us from Egypt by his constraining power,
subduing Pharao and his court with portents and
marvels, great and grievous, under our eyes. So rescued, he brought us here, and gave us entrance into
this fair land which he had promised to our fathers;
warning us that we must observe all these laws of his,
and go in fear of the Lord our God. Then the prosperity that is ours to-day will be ours all our life long;
he will have mercy on us, if he sees us ever faithful to
his commandments, ever obedient to his will.

READING II   Mk 12:28-34
A Reading from the Holy Gospel according to Mark

One of the scribes heard their dispute, and, finding
that he answered to the purpose, came up and asked
him, Which is the first commandment of all? Jesus
answered him, The first commandment of all is, Listen, Israel; there is no God but the Lord thy God; and
thou shalt love the Lord thy God with the love of thy
whole heart, and thy whole soul, and thy whole mind,
and thy whole strength. This is the first commandment, and the second, its like, is this, Thou shalt love
thy neighbour as thyself. There is no other commandment greater than these. And the scribe said to
him, Truly, Master, thou hast answered well; there is
but one God, and no other beside him; and if a man
loves God with all his heart and all his soul and all his
understanding and all his strength, and his
neighbour as himself, that is a greater thing than all
burnt-offerings and sacrifices. Then Jesus, seeing
how wisely he had answered, said to him, Thou art
not far from the kingdom of God. And after this, no
one dared to try him with further questions.

READING III   Rule of 1221, chaps. 22-23
A Reading from the Writings of St. Francis

We must all keep close watch over ourselves or we
will be lost and turn our minds and hearts from God,

because we think there is something worth having or doing, or that we will gain some advantage.

In that love which is God (cf. 1 Jn 4:16), I entreat all my friars, ministers and subjects, to put away every attachment, all care and solicitude, and serve, love, honour, and adore our Lord and God with a pure heart and mind; this is what he seeks above all else. We should make a dwelling-place within ourselves where he can stay, he who is the Lord God almighty, Father, Son, and Holy Spirit.

He himself tells us: *Watch, then, praying at all times, that you may be accounted worthy to escape all these things that are to be, and to stand before the Son of Man* (Lk 21:36). *When you stand up to pray* (Mk 11:25), say *Our Father who art in heaven* (Mt 6:9). Let us adore him with a pure heart for *we must always pray and not lose heart* (Lk 18:1); it is such men as these the Father claims for his worshippers. *God is spirit, and they who worship him must worship in spirit and truth* (Jn 4:24).

We should turn to him as to *the shepherd and guardian of our souls* (1 Pt 2:25). He says, *I am the good shepherd* (Jn 10:11). I feed my sheep and *I lay down my life for my sheep* (Jn 10:15). *All you are brothers. And call no one on earth your father; for one is your Father, who is in heaven.*

With all our hearts and all our souls, all our minds and all our strength, all our power and all our understanding, with every faculty (cf. Dt 6:5) and every effort, with every affection and all our emotions, with every wish and desire, we should love our Lord and God who has given and gives us everything, body and

soul, and all our life; it was he who created and redeemed us and of his mercy alone he will save us;
wretched and pitiable as we are, ungrateful and evil,
rotten through and through, he has provided us with
every good and does not cease to provide for us.

We should wish for nothing else and have no other
desire; we should find no pleasure or delight in anything except in our Creator, Redeemer, and Saviour;
he alone is true God, who is perfect good, all good,
every good, the true and supreme good, and he alone
is good, loving and gentle, kind and understanding;
he alone is holy, just, true, and right; he alone is kind,
innocent, pure, and from him, through him, and in
him is all pardon, all grace, and all glory for the peni-
tent, the just, and the blessed who rejoice in heaven.

Nothing, then, must keep us back, nothing separate
us from him, nothing come between us and him. At all
times and seasons, in every country and place, every
day and all day, we must have a true and humble
faith, and keep him in our hearts, where we must
love, honour, adore, serve, praise and bless, glorify
and acclaim, magnify and thank, the most high supreme and eternal God, Three and One, Father, Son,
and Holy Spirit, Creator of all and Saviour of those
who believe in him, who hope in him, and who love
him; without beginning and without end, he is un-
changeable, invisible, indescribable and ineffable, in-
comprehensible, unfathomable, blessed and worthy of
all praise, glorious, exalted, sublime, most high, kind,
lovable, delightful and utterly desirable beyond all
else, for ever and ever. (*Omnibus,* pp. 48-49, 51-52.)

2

MYSTERY OF THE CROSS

READING I   Is 52:13-53:12
A Reading from the Book of the Prophet Isaiah

See, here is my servant, one who will be prudent in
all his dealings. To what height he shall be raised,
how exalted, how extolled! So many there be that
stand gazing in horror; was ever a human form so
mishandled, human beauty ever so defaced? Yet this
is he that will purify a multitude of nations; kings
shall stand dumb in his presence; seen, now, where
men had no tidings of him, made known to such as
never heard his name.

What credence for such news as ours? Whom
reaches it, this new revelation of the Lord's strength?
He will watch this servant of his appear among us,
unregarded as brushwood shoot, as a plant in water-
less soil; no stateliness here, no majesty, no beauty, as
we gaze upon him, to win our hearts. Nay, here is one
despised, left out of all human reckoning; bowed with
misery, and no stranger to weakness; how should we
recognize that face? How should we take any account
of him, a man so despised? Our weakness, and it was
he who carried the weight of it, our miseries, and it
was he who bore them. A leper, so we thought of him,
a man God had smitten and brought low; and all the

18

while it was for our sins he was wounded, it was guilt
of ours crushed him down; on him the punishment fell
that brought us peace, by his bruises we were healed.
Strayed sheep all of us, each following his own path;
and God laid on his shoulders our guilt, the guilt of us
all.

A victim? Yet he himself bows to the stroke; no
word comes from him. Sheep led away to the
slaughter-house, lamb that stands dumb while it is
shorn; no word from him. Imprisoned, brought to
judgement, and carried off, he, whose birth is beyond
our knowing; numbered among the living no more! Be
sure it is for my people's guilt I have smitten him.
Takes he leave of the rich, the godless, to win but a
grave, to win but the gift of death; he, that wrong did
never, nor had treason on his lips! Ay, the Lord's will
it was, overwhelmed he should be with trouble. His
life laid down for guilt's atoning, he shall yet be rewarded; father of a long posterity, instrument of the
divine purpose; for all his heart's anguish, rewarded
in full. The Just One, my servant; many shall he
claim for his own, win their acquittal, on his shoulders bearing their guilt. So many lives ransomed, foes
so violent baulked of their spoil! Such is his due, that
gave himself up to death, and would be counted
among the wrong-doers; bore those many sins, and
made intercession for the guilty.

READING II   Mk 8:34-9:1
A Reading from the Holy Gospel according to Mark

And he called his disciples to him, and the multitude with them, and said to them, If any man has a mind to come my way, let him renounce self, and take up his cross, and follow me. The man who tries to save his life will lose it; it is the man who loses his life for my sake and for the gospel's sake, that will save it. How is a man the better for it, if he gains the whole world at the expense of losing his own soul? For a man's soul, what price can be high enough? If anyone is ashamed of acknowledging me and my words before this unfaithful and wicked generation, the Son of Man, when he comes in his Father's glory with the holy angels, will be ashamed to acknowledge him. Believe me, there are those standing here who will not taste of death before they have seen the kingdom of God present in all its power.

Six days afterwards, Jesus took Peter and James and John with him, and led them up to a high mountian where they were alone by themselves; and he was transfigured in their presence.

READING III   3 Soc., nos. 13-14
A Reading from the Life by the Three Companions

One day while Francis was fervently imploring God's mercy, the Lord revealed to him that he would shortly be taught what he was to do. From that moment he was so full of joy that, beside himself for gladness, he would let fall occasional words of his secret for men to hear.

A few days after this, while he was walking near the church of San Damiano, an inner voice bade him go in and pray. He obeyed, and kneeling before an image of the crucified Savior, he began to pray most devoutly. A tender, compassionate voice then spoke to him: "Francis, do you not see that my house is falling into ruin? Go, and repair it for me." Trembling and amazed Francis replied: "Gladly I will do so, O Lord." He had understood that the Lord was speaking of that very church which, on account of its age, was indeed falling into ruin.

These words filled him with the greatest joy and inner light because in spirit he knew that it was indeed Jesus Christ who had spoken to him. On leaving the church he found the priest who had charge of it sitting outside, and taking a handful of money from his purse, he said: "I beg you, Sir, to buy oil and keep the lamp before this image of Christ constantly alight. When this is spent I will give you as much as you need."

From that hour his heart was stricken and wounded with melting love and compassion for the passion of Christ; and for the rest of his life he carried in it the wounds of the Lord Jesus. This was clearly proved later when the stigmata of those same wounds were miraculously impressed upon his own holy body for all to see. Henceforth he continually mortified his body most harshly, not only when he was well, but also when he was ill. Seldom indeed did he relax this severity; so much so, that on his deathbed he confessed to having sinned grievously against Brother Body.

One day he was roaming about alone near the church of Saint Mary of the Angels, weeping and lamenting aloud. A certain God-fearing man heard him and, thinking he must be ill, asked pityingly the reason for his distress. Francis replied: "I weep for the passion of my Lord Jesus Christ; and I should not be ashamed to go weeping through the whole world for his sake." Then the other man fell to crying and lamenting with him.

Often when he rose from prayer we saw that his eyes were inflamed and red from his bitter weeping. Besides shedding these abundant tears, Francis also abstained in memory of our Lord's passion from eating and drinking. (*Omnibus*, pp. 903-904.)

3

WAY OF LIFE

READING I   Ex 24:1-8
A Reading from the Book of Exodus

Then Moses was told, Do thou and Aaron and
Nadab and Abiu, with seventy elders of Israel, come
up to meet the Lord, and worship from afar. Only
Moses must enter the Lord's presence, the rest are not
to draw near, and none of the people are to come up
with him. So Moses went and told the people all the
Lord had said, all the commands he had given; and
the whole people answered with one voice, We will do
all that the Lord has bidden us. Then Moses committed everything the Lord had said to writing; and when
he rose next morning, he built an altar close to the
spurs of the mountain, and twelve memorial stones
answering to the twelve tribes of Israel. And he di-
rected some of the younger Israelites to make burnt-
sacrifice there and bring welcome-offerings to the
Lord, with bullocks for their victims. After this Moses
took half of the blood, and set it aside in bowls; the
other half he poured out on the altar. Then he took up
the book in which the covenant was inscribed, and
read it aloud to the people. We will do all the Lord has
bidden us, said they; we promise obedience; and
Moses took the blood and sprinkled it over the people,

crying out, Here is the blood of the covenant which
the Lord makes with you, in accordance with all these
words of his.

READING II   Mt 5; 1-16
A Reading from the Holy Gospel according to
Matthew

Jesus, when he saw how great was their number,
went up on to the mountainside; there he sat down,
and his disciples came about him. And he began
speaking to them; this was the teaching he gave.
Blessed are the poor in spirit; the kingdom of heaven
is theirs. Blessed are the patient; they shall inherit
the land. Blessed are those who mourn; they shall be
comforted. Blessed are those who hunger and thirst
for holiness; they shall have their fill. Blessed are the
merciful; they shall obtain mercy. Blessed are the
clean of heart; they shall see God. Blessed are the
peace-makers; they shall be counted the children of
God. Blessed are those who suffer persecution in the
cause of right; the kingdom of heaven is theirs. Blessed are you, when men revile you, and persecute you,
and speak all manner of evil against you falsely, because of me. Be glad and light-hearted, for a rich reward awaits you in heaven; so it was they persecuted
the prophets who went before you. You are the salt of
the earth; if salt loses its taste, what is there left to
give taste to it? There is no more to be done with it,

but throw it out of doors for men to tread it under foot.
You are the light of the world; a city cannot be hidden
if it is built on a mountain-top. A lamp is not lighted
to be put away under a bushel measure; it is put on
the lamp-stand, to give light to all the people of the
house; and your light must shine so brightly before
men that they can see your good works, and glorify
your Father who is in heaven.

READING III   Testament
A Reading from the Writings of St. Francis

When God gave me some friars, there was no one to
tell me what I should do; but the Most High himself
made it clear to me that I must live the life of the
Gospel. I had this written down briefly and simply
and his holiness the Pope confirmed it for me. Those
who embraced this life gave everything they had to
the poor. They were satisfied with one habit which
was patched inside and outside, and a cord, and trous-
ers. We refused to have anything more.

Those of us who were clerics said the Office like
other clerics, while the lay brothers said the *Our
Father*, and we were only too glad to find shelter in
abandoned churches. We made no claim to learning
and we were submissive to everyone. I worked with
my own hands and I am still determined to work; and
with all my heart I want all the other friars to be busy
with some kind of work that can be carried on without

scandal. Those who do not know how to work should learn, not because they want to get something for their efforts, but to give good example and to avoid idleness. When we receive no recompense for our work, we can turn to God's table and beg alms from door to door. God revealed a form of greeting to me, telling me that we should say, "God give you peace."

The friars must be very careful not to accept churches or poor dwellings for themselves, or anything else built for them, unless they are in harmony with the poverty which we have promised in the Rule; and they should occupy these places only as strangers and pilgrims.

In virtue of obedience, I strictly forbid the friars, wherever they may be, to petition the Roman Curia, either personally or through an intermediary, for a papal brief, whether it concerns a church or any other place, or even in order to preach, or because they are being persecuted. If they are not welcome somewhere, they should flee to another country where they can lead a life of penance, with God's blessing.

I am determined to obey the Minister General of the Order and the guardian whom he sees fit to give me. I want to be a captive in his hands so that I cannot travel about or do anything against his command or desire, because he is my superior. Although I am ill and not much use, I always want to have a cleric with me who will say the Office for me, as is prescribed in the Rule.

All the other friars, too, are bound to obey their guardians in the same way, and say the Office according to the Rule.

And may whoever observes all this be filled in heaven with the blessing of the most high Father, and on earth with that of his beloved Son, together with the Holy Spirit, the Comforter, and all the powers of heaven and all the saints. And I, Brother Francis, your poor worthless servant, add my share internally and externally to that most holy blessing. Amen. (*Omnibus*, pp. 68-70.)

4

TO OBSERVE THE HOLY GOSPEL
OF OUR LORD JESUS CHRIST

READING I   2 Cor 4:7-15
A Reading from the Second Letter of Paul to the
Corinthians

We have a treasure, then, in our keeping, but its
shell is of perishable earthenware; it must be God,
and not anything in ourselves, that gives it its sover-
eign power. For ourselves, we are being hampered
everywhere, yet still have room to breathe, are hard
put to it, but never at a loss; persecution does not
leave us unbefriended, nor crushing blows destroy us;
we carry about continually in our bodies the dying
state of Jesus, so that the living power of Jesus may
be manifested in our bodies too. Always we, alive as
we are, are being given up to death for Jesus' sake, so
that the living power of Jesus may be manifested in
this mortal nature of ours. So death makes itself felt
in us, and life in you. I spoke my mind, says the scripture, with full confidence, and we too speak our minds
with full confidence, sharing that same spirit of faith,
and knowing that he who raised Jesus from the dead
will raise us too, and summon us, like you, before
him. It is all for your sakes, so that grace made manifold in many lives may increase the sum of gratitude

which is offered to God's glory. No, we do not play the coward; though the outward part of our nature is being worn down, our inner life is refreshed from day to day.

READING II   Mt 10:5-16
A Reading from the Holy Gospel according to
Matthew

These twelve Jesus sent out; but first gave them their instructions; Do not go, he said, into the walks of the Gentiles, or enter any city of Samaria; go rather to the lost sheep that belong to the house of Israel. And preach as you go, telling them, The kingdom of heaven is at hand. Heal the sick, raise the dead, cleanse the lepers, cast out devils: give as you have received the gift, without payment. Do not provide gold or silver or copper to fill your purses, nor a wallet for the journey, no second coat, no spare shoes or staff; the labourer has a right to his maintenance. Whenever you enter a city or a village, find out who is worthy to be your host, and make your lodging there until you go away. When you enter this house, you are to wish it well; and so, if the house is worthy, your good wishes shall come down upon it; if unworthy, let them come back to you the way they went. And wherever they will not receive you or listen to your words, shake off the dust from your feet as you leave that city or that house; I promise you, it shall go less hard with the land of Sodom and Gomorrha at the day of judgement, than with that city.

Remember, I am sending you out to be like sheep among wolves; you must be wary, then, as serpents, and yet innocent as doves.

READING III   Expos., chap. I
A Reading from Fr. Hugh of Digne's
Exposition of the Rule

What else is the Rule if not a kind of Summary of Gospel perfection? For however perfect the Rule which the Apostles gave to the primitive Church and which the Founders of Religious Orders later on took up, this was especially so with the Rule which Saint Francis gave to his Friars, which Christ himself had given to his Apostles, embracing both the teaching and the life of the Gospel.

For the entire longing and endeavor of Saint Francis and of his primitive followers was to observe the Gospel. Both their words and their deeds proved that they were truly followers of the Gospel, as I shall show by a few examples. They had on their lips the word and greeting of peace, which Blessed Francis had learned from the example of Christ and through his revelation, as he himself testifies in the words: "The Lord revealed to me this salutation, that we should say 'The Lord give you peace!'" They detested oaths and assurances, such as certain undisciplined persons in the world employ frequently as a matter of course; but their words were simply "Yes, yes" or "No, no"—as the Gospel recommends.

While going about in the world, they were fully satisfied with whatever fare the people could offer them,—in accordance with the teaching of the Gospel; and in order not to accept food without making any recompense, they repaid their benefactors with the nourishment of the Word of God, bringing forth things new and old from their storehouse of a good conscience. Whenever they entered a house, they brought in with them not the curse of worldliness and buffoonery, but the blessing of holy conversation and good example.

In accordance with the norm set down in the Gospel, they avoided bestowing on each other any titles of honor, and none of them in the Order was called Master or Lord. They considered it wrong to address a confrere with the insulting epithet of "Raca" or "Thou fool," since the earlier Rule had incorporated these very words from the Gospel.

If they had offered anyone the slightest cause to take offence, they immediately—before offering their gift of prayer to the Lord or before trying to go to sleep—strove to become reconciled to their Brother. The Gospel precept of mutual love they observed so perfectly that they treated each other as a mother would treat her own child.

In accordance with the Gospel teaching, they shunned all cares and worries of this world and did not become involved in external affairs, They did not resist the evildoer, nor did they demand back their own, nor did they contend in court. Whatever could be evil or could have the appearance of evil or be the occasion for evil—however useful it might seem to be—they most resolutely avoided; and if their hand or their eye—no matter how necessary for them—scandalized them, they mystically but courageously cut them off.

They were truly poor in spirit, meek, merciful, peaceful, and in a remarkable manner avoided giving the least scandal to anyone. How through the cross of penance they strive to enter through the narrow gate, how through mortification of the flesh by means of fasting and abstinence, through vigilance and prayer and various labors they tortured themselves,—that could not be adequately described in a few words.

By these and similar examples of our forefathers we are encouraged to the same practices. For it is surely becoming that those who profess the Gospel, should also (as far as it is possible for the perfect in imitation of the Saints) become perfect observers of the Gospel.

5

LIFE OF THE CHURCH
IN THE PEOPLE OF GOD

READING I   Eph 3:1-12
A Reading from the Letter of Paul to the Ephesians

With this in mind, I fall on my knees; I, Paul, of whom Jesus Christ has made a prisoner for the love of you Gentiles. You will have been told how God planned to give me a special grace for preaching to you; how a revelation taught me the secret I have been setting out briefly here; briefly, yet so as to let you see how well I have mastered this secret of Christ's. It was never made known to any human being in past ages, as it has now been revealed by the Spirit to his holy apostles and prophets, and it is this: that through the gospel preaching the Gentiles are to win the same inheritance, to be made part of the same body, to share the same divine promise, in Christ Jesus. With what grace God gives me (and he gives it in all the effectiveness of his power), I am a minister of that gospel; on me, least as I am of all the saints, he has bestowed this privilege, of making known to the Gentiles the unfathomable riches of Christ, of publishing to the world the plan of this mystery, kept hidden from the beginning of time in the all-creating mind of God. The principalities and powers of heaven are to see, now, made manifest in the Church, the

subtlety of God's wisdom; such is his eternal purpose,
centred in Christ Jesus our Lord, who gives us all our
confidence, bids us come forward, emboldened by our
faith in him.

READING II   Mk 16: 15-20
A Reading from the Holy Gospel according to Mark

He said to them, Go out all over the world and preach
the gospel to the whole creation; he who believes
and is baptized will be saved; he who refuses belief
will be condemned. Where believers go, these signs
shall go with them; they will cast out devils in my
name, they will speak in tongues that are strange
to them; they will take up serpents in their hands,
and drink poisonous draughts without harm; they
will lay their hands upon the sick and make them
recover. And so the Lord Jesus, when he had finished
speaking to them, was taken up to heaven, and is
seated now at the right hand of God; and they went
out and preached everywhere, the Lord aiding them,
and attesting his word by the miracles that went with
them.

READING III   Cel. I, no. 89, II, no. 148
A Reading from the Lives by Fr. Thomas of Celano

Francis was sent by God to bear *witness to the truth*
throughout the whole world in accordance with the
example of the Apostles. And thus it came to pass that

his teaching showed that *the wisdom of this world* is
most evidently *turned to foolishness,* and within a
short period of time brought it, under the guidance of
Christ, to the true widom of God *by the foolishness of*
his *preaching.* For in this *last time* this new
evangelist, like one of the rivers that flowed out of
paradise, diffused the waters of the Gospel over the
whole world by his tender watering, and preached by
his deeds the way of the Son of God and the doctrine of
truth. Accordingly, in him and through him there
arose throughout the world an unlooked for happiness
and a holy newness, and a shoot of the ancient religion suddenly brought a great renewal to those who
had grown calloused and to the very old. A new spirit
was born in the hearts of the elect, and a saving unc-
tion was poured out in their midst, when the servant
and holy man of Christ, like one of the lights of the
heavens, shone brilliantly with a new rite and with
new signs. Through him the miracles of ancient times
were renewed, while there was planted in the desert
of this world, by a new order but in an ancient way, a
fruitful vine bearing flowers of sweetness unto the
odor of holy virtues by extending everywhere the
branches of a sacred religion.

Those two bright lights of the world, St. Dominic
and St. Francis, were together in Rome once with the
lord of Ostia, who later became the supreme pontiff.
And after they had spoken affectionate words in turn
about the Lord, the bishop finally said to them: "In
the primitive church the pastors of the church were
poor and were men of charity, not men of greed.
Why," he said, "do we not in the future make bishops

and prelates from among your brothers who excel all others by their learning and example?" A dispute followed between the saints as to which one should answer; they both strove not to anticipate each other but to give way to each other; what is more, each was urging the other to make the reply. Each one gave preference to the other, for each one was devoted to the other. But in the end, humility conquered Francis, lest he put himself forward; and humility conquered Dominic, so that he would humbly obey and answer first. Therefore, replying, the blessed Dominic said to the bishop: "Lord, my brothers have been raised to a high station, if they only knew it; and even if I wanted to, I could not permit them to acquire any other dignity." After he had replied thus briefly, the blessed Francis bowed before the bishop and said: "Lord, my brothers are called *minors* so that they will not presume to become greater. Their vocation teaches them to remain in a lowly station and to follow the footsteps of the humble Christ, so that in the end they may be exalted above the rest in the sight of the saints. If," he said, "you want them to bear fruit for the church of God, hold them and preserve them in the station to which they have been called, and bring them back to a lowly station, even if they are unwilling. I pray you, therefore, Father, that you by no means permit them to rise to any prelacy, lest they become prouder rather than poorer and grow arrogand toward rest." (*Omnibus,* pp. 304, 481–482.)

6

ASSISTING THE CLERGY
AT THE FEET OF THE HOLY CHURCH

READING I Rom 12:4-16
A Reading from the Letter of Paul to the Romans

Each of us has one body, with many different parts, and not all these parts have the same function; just so we, though many in number, form one body in Christ, and each acts as the counterpart of another. The spiritual gifts we have differ, according to the special grace which has been assigned to each. If a man is a prophet, let him prophesy as far as the measure of his faith will let him. The administrator must be content with his administration, the teacher, with his work of teaching, the preacher, with his preaching. Each must perform his own task well; giving alms with generosity, exercising authority with anxious care, or doing works of mercy smilingly.

Your love must be a sincere love; you must hold what is evil in abomination, fix all your desire upon what is good. Be affectionate towards each other, as the love of brothers demands, eager to give one another precedence. I would see you unwearied in activity, aglow with the Spirit, waiting like slaves upon the Lord; buoyed up by hope, patient in affliction, persevering in prayer; providing generously for the

needs of the saints, giving the stranger a loving welcome. Bestow a blessing on those who persecute you; a
blessing, not a curse. Rejoice with those who rejoice,
mourn with the mourner. Live in harmony of mind,
falling in with the opinions of common folk, instead of
following conceited thoughts; never give yourselves
airs of wisdom.

READING II   Lk 10:1-11, 16
A Reading from the Holy Gospel according to Luke

After this, the Lord appointed seventy-two others,
and sent them before him, two and two, into all the
cities and villages he himself was to visit. The harvest, he told them, is plentiful enough, but the
labourers are few; you must ask the Lord to whom the
harvest belongs to send labourers out for the harvest-
ing. Go then, and remember, I am sending you out to
be like lambs among wolves. You are not to carry
purse, or wallet, or shoes; you are to give no one greeting on your way. When you enter a house, say first of
all, Peace be to this house; and if those who dwell
there are men of good will, your good wishes shall
come down upon it; if not, they will come back to you
the way they went. Remain in the same house, eating
and drinking what they have to give you; the labourer
has a right to his maintenance; do not move from one
house to another. When you enter a city, and they
make you welcome, be content to eat the fare they
offer you: and heal those who are sick there; and tell

them, The kingdom of God is close upon you. But if you enter a city where they will not make you welcome, go out into their streets, and say, We brush off in your faces the very dust from your city that has clung to our feet; and be sure of this, the kingdom of God is close at hand.

He who listens to you, listens to me; he who despises you, despises me; and he who despises me, despises him that sent me.

READING III   Cel. I, no. 62; II, no. 146
A Reading from the Lives by Fr. Thomas of Celano

So great was the faith of the men and women, so great their devotion toward the holy man of God, that he pronounced himself happy who could but touch his garment. When he entered any city, the clergy rejoiced, the bells were rung, the men were filled with happiness, the women rejoiced together, the children clapped their hands; and often, taking branches from the trees, they went to meet him singing. The wickedness of heretics was confounded, the faith of the Church exalted; and while the faithful rejoiced, the heretics slipped secretly away. For such great signs of sanctity were evident in him that no one dared to oppose his words, while the great assembly of people looked only upon him. In the midst of all these things and above everything else, Francis thought that the faith of the holy Roman Church was by all means to be preserved, honored, and imitated, that faith in

which alone is found the salvation of all who are to be
saved. He revered priests and he had a great affection
for every ecclesiastical order. . . .

But, though Francis wanted his sons to *be at peace
with all men* and to conduct themselves as little ones
among all, he taught by his words and showed by his
example that they were to be especially humble toward clerics. For he used to say: "We have been sent
to help the clergy toward the salvation of souls so that
what might be found insufficient in them might be
supplied by us. Everyone will receive his reward, not
according to the authority he exercises, but according
to the labor he does. Know, brothers," he said, "the
fruit of souls is most pleasing to God, and it can be
better obtained by peace with clerics than by dis-
agreements with them. If they hinder the salvation of
people, the revenge pertains to God and he will *repay
them in due time.* Therefore, be subject to prelates, so
that, in so far as you can help it, no jealousy will
spring up. If you will be sons of peace, you will win the
clergy and the people for the Lord, and the Lord
judges this more acceptable than to win the people
but scandalize the clergy. Hide their lapses, supply
for their many defects; and when you have done this,
be even more humble." (*Omnibus,* pp. 281, 479-480.)

7

LOVE OF GOD

READING I   Rom. 8:28-39
A Reading from the Letter of Paul to the Romans

Meanwhile, we are well assured that everything helps to secure the good of those who love God, those whom he has called in fulfilment of his design. All those who from the first were known to him, he has destined from the first to be moulded into the image of his Son, who is thus to become the eldest-born among many brethren. So predestined, he called them; so called, he justified them; so justified, he glorified them. When that is said, what follows? Who can be our adversary, if God is on our side? He did not even spare his own Son, but gave him up for us all; and must not that gift be accompanied by the gift of all else? Who will come forward to accuse God's elect, when God acquits us? Who will pass sentence against us, when Jesus Christ, who died, nay, has risen again, and sits at the right hand of God, is pleading for us? Who will separate us from the love of Christ? Will affliction, or distress, or persecution, or hunger, or nakedness, or peril, or the sword? For thy sake, says the scripture, we face death at every moment, reckoned no better than sheep marked down for slaughter. Yet in all this we are conquerors, through him who has granted us

41

his love. Of this I am fully persuaded; neither death
nor life, no angels or principalities or powers, neither
what is present nor what is to come, no force whatever, neither the height above us nor the depth beneath us, nor any other created thing, will be able to
separate us from the love of God, which comes to us in
Christ Jesus our Lord.

READING II   Jn 15:9-17
A Reading from the Holy Gospel according to John

I have bestowed my love upon you, just as my
Father has bestowed his love upon me; live on, then,
in my love. You will live on in my love, if you keep my
commandments, just as it is by keeping my Father's
commandments that I live on in his love.

All this I have told you, so that my joy may be
yours, and the measure of your joy may be filled up.
This is my commandment, that you should love one
another, as I have loved you. This is the greatest love
a man can shew, that he should lay down his life for
his friends; and you, if you do all that I command you,
are my friends. I do not speak of you any more as my
servants; a servant is one who does not understand
what his master is about, whereas I have made
known to you all that my Father has told me; and so I
have called you my friends. It was not you that chose
me, it was I that chose you. The task I have appointed
you is to go out and bear fruit, fruit which will endure; so that every request you make of the Father in

my name may be granted you. These are the directions I give you, that you should love one another.

READING III   Letter III to Bl. Agnes of Prague
A Reading from the Writings of St. Clare

May you, dearest Sister, always rejoice in the Lord, and may you, most dearly beloved Lady in Christ, the joy of the angels and the crown of Sisters, never be enveloped in bitterness and in a cloud of darkness. Behold your mind in the mirror of eternity, place your soul in the splendor of heavenly glory, fix your heart in the form of the Divine Substance, and transform yourself entirely by contemplating the image of God Himself, so that you also will experience what God's friends feel in enjoying that hidden delight which God has from all eternity prepared for those who love him.

And completely despising the allurements with which this fickle and changeable world ensnares its blind devotees, may you with your whole being love Him who offered himself entirely out of love for you; Him, whose beauty the sun and the moon admire, whose rewards are infinitely precious and great; I say, love that Son of the Most High, whom the Virgin brought forth, yet remaining a Virgin after his birth. Cling to that most lovable Mother, who gave birth to a Son so great that the Heavens could not contain Him,—and yet she enclosed Him within the narrow chamber of her sacred womb and carried Him within her maiden breast.

Who would not abhor the wiles of the enemy of mankind, who through an endless succession of momentary and fleeting glories would force man to disregard Him who is above the Heavens?

Behold it is now evident that through God's grace the most worthy of all creatures—the soul of a believer—is greater than Heaven itself. For Heaven and all of creation cannot contain the Creator, yet the soul of the faithful alone becomes His resting-place and home, and this only by virtue of that love which the wicked lack; for the Truth proclaims: "He who loves me, will be loved by my Father, and I will love him; and we will come to him and make our abode with him."

Therefore, as the Virgin of virgins in a material way, so also you in a spiritual way—by following in her footsteps, especially through humility and poverty—can in a chaste and virginal body always and most assuredly bear all things, since you embrace Him, in whom you yourself and all created things are contained; since you possess Him who is far superior when compared with all transitory possessions of this world.

Certain kings and queens of this world deceive themselves; for although their pride may have risen up to Heaven and their heads may have touched the clouds, they finally perish like a dung-heap.

8

LOVE OF NEIGHBOR

READING I   1 Cor 13:1-13

A Reading from the Second Letter of Paul to the
Corinthians

I may speak with every tongue that men and angels
use; yet, if I lack charity, I am no better than echoing
bronze, or the clash of cymbals. I may have powers of
prophecy, no secret hidden from me, no knowledge too
deep for me; I may have utter faith, so that I can move
mountains; yet if I lack charity, I count for nothing. I
may give away all that I have, to feed the poor; I may
give myself up to be burnt at the stake; if I lack charity, it goes for nothing. Charity is patient, is kind;
charity feels no envy; charity is never perverse or
proud, never insolent; does not claim its rights, cannot
be provoked, does not brood over an injury; takes no
pleasure in wrong-doing, but rejoices at the victory of
truth; sustains, believes, hopes, endures, to the last.
The time will come when we shall outgrow prophecy,
when speaking with tongues will come to an end,
when knowledge will be swept away; we shall never
have finished with charity. Our knowledge, our
prophecy, are only glimpses of the truth; and these
glimpses will be swept away when the time of fulfilment comes. (Just so, when I was a child, I talked like

45

a child, I had the intelligence, the thoughts of a child;
since I became a man, I have outgrown childish
ways.) At present, we are looking at a confused reflec-
tion in a mirror; then, we shall see face to face; now, I
have only glimpses of knowledge; then, I shall recognize God as he has recognized me. Meanwhile, faith,
hope and charity persist, all three; but the greatest of
them all is charity.

READING II   Lk 6:27-28
A Reading from the Holy Gospel according to Luke

And now I say to you who are listening to me, Love
your enemies, do good to those who hate you; bless
those who curse you, and pray for those who treat you
insultingly.

READING III   Rule of 1221, Letter to All the Faithful
A Reading from the Writings of St. Francis

Far from indulging in detraction or disputing in
words (2 Tim 2: 14) the friars should do their best to
avoid talking, according as God gives them the opportunity. There must be no quarrelling among themselves or with others, and they should be content to
answer everyone humbly, saying, *We are unprofitable
servants* (Lk 17: 10). They must not give way to anger

because the Gospel says: *Everyone who is angry with his brother shall be liable to judgment; and whoever says to his brother, "Raca," shall be liable to the Sanhedrin; and whoever says, "Thou fool," shall be liable to the fire of Gehenna* (Mt 5: 22).

The friars are bound to love one another because our Lord says, *This is my commandment, that you love one another as I have loved you* (Jn 15: 12). And they must prove their love by deeds, as St John says: *Let us not love in word, neither with the tongue, but in deed and in truth* (1 Jn 3: 18).

They are to speak *evil of none* (Tit 3: 2); there must be no complaining, no slander; it is written, "Whisperers and detractors are people hateful to God" (cf. Rom 1: 29). And let them be *moderate, showing all mildness to all men* (Tit 3: 2), without a word of criticism or condemnation; as our Lord says, they must give no thought even to the slightest faults of others (cf. Mt 7: 3; Lk 6: 41), but rather count over their own in the bitterness of their soul (cf. Is 38: 15). They must *strive to enter by the narrow gate* (Lk 13: 24), because in the words of the Gospel, *How narrow the gate and close the way that leads to life! And few there are who find it* (Mt 7: 14). . . .

We must love our neighbors as ourselves. Anyone who will not or cannot love his neighbor as himself should at least do him good and not do him any harm.

Those who have been entrusted with the power of judging others should pass judgement mercifully, just as they themselves hope to obtain mercy from God. *For judgement is without mercy to him who has not shown mercy* (Ja 2: 13). We must be charitable, too, and humble, and give alms, because they wash the stains of sin from our souls. We lose everything which we leave behind us in this world; we can bring with us only the right to a reward for our charity and the alms we have given. For these we shall receive a reward, a just retribution from God. (*Omnibus,* pp. 41, 94-95.)

9

ASSIDUOUS WORK

READING I 2 Thes 3:6-12, 16
A Reading from the Second Letter of Paul to the Thessalonians

Only, brethren, we charge you in the name of our Lord Jesus Christ to have nothing to do with any brother who lives a vagabond life, contrary to the tradition which we handed on; you do not need to be reminded how, on our visit, we set you an example to be imitated; we were no vagabonds ourselves. We would not even be indebted to you for our daily bread, we earned it in weariness and toil, working with our hands, night and day, so as not to be a burden to any of you; not that we are obliged to do so, but as a model for your own behaviour; you were to follow our example. The charge we gave you on our visit was that the man who refuses to work must be left to starve. And now we are told that there are those among you who live in idleness, neglecting their own business to mind other people's. We charge all such, we appeal to them in the Lord Jesus Christ, to earn their bread by going on calmly with their work.

And may the Lord of peace grant you peace everywhere and at all times; the Lord be with you all.

READING II   Mt 6:31-34
A Reading from the Holy Gospel according to
Matthew

Do not fret, then asking, What are we to eat? or
What are we to drink? or How shall we find clothing?
It is for the heathen to busy themselves over such
things; you have a Father in heaven who knows that
you need them all. Make it your first care to find the
kingdom of God, and his approval, and all these
things shall be yours without the asking. Do not fret,
then, over to-morrow; leave to-morrow to fret over its
own needs; for to-day, to-day's troubles are enough.

READING III   Cel. I, no. 39; II, nos. 161, 162
A Reading from the Lives by Fr. Thomas of Celano

During the day, those who knew how labored with
their hands, staying in the houses of lepers, or in
other decent places, serving all humbly and de-
votedly. They did not wish to exercise any position
from which scandal might arise, but always doing
what is holy and just, honest and useful, they led all
with whom they came into contact to follow their
example of humility and patience.

Holy Father, permit us who are called your sons to
raise on high today a lament. The exercise of virtue is
odious to many who, wanting to rest before they have
labored, prove themselves to be sons of Lucifer rather
than sons of Francis. We have a greater abundance of

weaklings than of warriors, although they ought to
consider this life a warfare, since they have been born
to labor. It does not please them to make progress
through action; and they cannot do so through contemplation. When they have disturbed all by their
singularity, working more with their jaws than with
their hands, they hate *him that rebuketh them in the
gate,* and they do not permit themselves to be touched
even by the tips of the fingers. But I wonder still more
at the impudence of those who, according to the word
of the blessed Francis, could not have lived at home
except by their sweat, and now, without working, feed
on the sweat of the poor. Wonderful prudence! Though
they do nothing, they consider themselves always oc-
cupied. They know the hours of the meals, and if
hunger takes hold of them, they complain that the
sun has gone to sleep. Shall I believe, good Father,
that these monsters of men are worthy of your glory?
Not even of the habit! You always taught that we
should seek in this wanton and fleeting time the
riches of merits, lest it happen that we go begging in
the future. These, though, have no part in their
fatherland, and they will have to go into exile hereaf-
ter. This disease is rampant among subjects because
superiors act as though it were not possible to merit a
share in the punishment of those whose vices they are
tolerating. (*Omnibus,* pp. 262, 492.)

10

LOVING CARE OF SOULS
BY EXAMPLE MORE THAN BY WORD

READING I   1 Cor. 2:1-10
A Reading from the First Letter of Paul to the Corinthians

So it was, brethren, that when I came to you and preached Christ's message to you, I did so without any high pretensions to eloquence, or to philosophy. I had no thought of bringing you any other knowledge than that of Jesus Christ, and of him as crucified. It was with distrust of myself, full of anxious fear, that I approached you; my preaching, my message depended on no persuasive language, devised by human wisdom, but rather on the proof I gave you of spiritual power; God's power, not man's wisdom, was to be the foundation of your faith.

There is, to be sure, a wisdom which we make known among those who are fully grounded; but it is not the wisdom of this world, or of this world's rulers, whose power is to be abrogated. What we make known is the wisdom of God, his secret, kept hidden til now; so, before the ages, God had decreed, reserving glory for us. (None of the rulers of this world could read his secret, or they would not have crucified him to whom all glory belongs.) So we read of, Things no eye has seen, no ear has heard, no human heart conceived, the welcome God has prepared for those who love him. To us, then, God has made a revelation of it through his Spirit; there is no depth in God's nature so deep that the Spirit cannot find it out.

READING II   Jn 17:11, 17-23
A Reading from the Holy Gospel according to John

I am remaining in the world no longer, but they remain in the world, while I am on my way to thee. Holy Father, keep them true to thy name, thy gift to me, that they may be one, as we are one.

Keep them holy, then, through the truth; it is thy word that is truth. Thou has sent me into the world on thy errand, and I have sent them into the world on my errand; and I dedicate myself for their sakes, that they too may be dedicated through the truth.

It is not only for them that I pray; I pray for those who are to find faith in me through their word; that they may all be one; that they too may be one in us, as thou Father, art in me, and I in thee; so that the world may come to believe that it is thou who hast sent me. And I have given them the privilege which thou gavest to me, that they should all be one, as we are one; that while thou art in me, I may be in them, and so they may be perfectly made one. So let the world know that it is thou who hast sent me, and that thou hast bestowed thy love upon them, as thou hast bestowed it upon me.

A Reading from the Life by the Three Companions

From this time onward Saint Francis wandered
through cities, villages, and hamlets, and began to
preach with increasing perfection, not using learned
words of human wisdom, but through the doctrine
and virtue of the Holy Spirit most confidently pro-
claiming the kingdom of God. He was a genuine
preacher confirmed by apostolic authority; therefore
he spoke no honeyed words of flattery or blandish-
ment; what he preached to others he had already put
into practice himself and his teaching of the truth was
full of assurance. The power and truth of what he said
did not come from any human source; and his words
impressed many learned and cultured men who hastened to see and hear him as though he were a being
from another century. Many of the people, nobles and
commoners alike, were touched by divine inspiration
and began to imitate Francis' way of life, and to follow
in his steps. They abandoned the cares and pomps of
the world, desiring to live under his direction, guidance, and discipline.

Blessed Francis also warned his brothers never to
judge or criticize those who live in luxury, eat fastidi-
ously, and indulge in superfluous and splendid
clothes; God, he said, is their Lord and ours; he has
the power to call them to himself and to justify them.
He insisted that the friars should reverence such men
as their brothers and masters, and they are indeed
brothers since they are children of the same Creator;
while they are our masters since they help the good to

do penance by giving them what is necessary to the body. To this blessed Francis added: "The general behavior of the friars among people must be such that all who see or hear them may be drawn to glorify our heavenly Father and to praise him devoutly." His great desire was that he and his brothers should abound in the good works for which men give glory and praise to God.

He also said to the brothers: "Since you speak of peace, all the more so must you have it in your hearts. Let none be provoked to anger or scandal by you, but rather may they be drawn to peace and good will, to benignity and concord through your gentleness. We have been called to heal wounds, to unite what has fallen apart, and to bring home those who have lost their way. Many who may seem to us to be children of the Devil will still become Christ's disciples."

Besides insisting on these things, the kind father reproved his brothers when they were too harsh on themselves, wearing out their strength in excessive vigils, fasts, and corporal penance. Some of them mortified their bodies so severely in order to repress all the natural human impulses that they appeared to be hating themselves. Francis being filled with the wisdom and grace of our Savior, reproached the brothers gently for all this and, using rational arguments, he forbade such excesses, binding up their wounds with the bandages of sane precepts and directions.

None of the friars assembled at the chapter ever dared to recount any worldly events: they spoke together of the lives of the holy fathers of old, and how

they might best live in God's grace. If by chance anyone among those present was troubled or tempted, the
very sight of blessed Francis and his fervent and gentle exhortations were sufficient to drive away all
temptation and trouble. He spoke indeed not as judge
but as a tender father to his children, as a kind doctor
to his patients; he suffered with the sick, and grieved
with those in tribulation. Nevertheless he knew how
to reprove evildoers and to impose discipline on the
obstinate and rebellious.

At the end of the chapter he blessed all the friars
and assigned to each his province; he gave permission
to preach to anyone who had the spirit of God and the
necessary eloquence, whether cleric or brother. When
all present had received his blessing, in great joy of
spirit they started on their way through the world as
pilgrims and strangers, taking nothing with them for
the journey except their office book.

Whenever they came on a priest, rich or poor, good
or bad, they bowed humbly before him; and when it
was time to seek shelter for the night they preferred
to lodge with priests sooner than with layfolk. (*Omnibus,* pp. 938, 942–943.)

11

OBEDIENCE ACCORDING TO
THE MIND OF ST. FRANCIS

READING I   Phil 2:5-13
A Reading from the Letter of Paul to the Philippians

Yours is to be the same mind which Christ Jesus shewed. His nature is, from the first, divine, and yet he did not see, in the rank of Godhead, a prize to be coveted; he dispossessed himself, and took the nature of a slave, fashioned in the likeness of men, and presenting himself to us in human form; and then he lowered his own dignity, accepted an obedience which brought him to death, death on a cross. That is why God has raised him to such a height, given him that name which is greater than any other name; so that everything in heaven and on earth and under the earth must bend the knee before the name of Jesus, and every tongue must confess Jesus Christ as the Lord, dwelling in the glory of God the Father.

Beloved, you have always shewn yourselves obedient; and now that I am at a distance, not less but much more than when I am present, you must work to earn your salvation, in anxious fear. Both the will to do it and the accomplishment of that will are something which God accomplishes in you, to carry out his loving purpose.

READING II   Mk 3:31-35
A Reading from the Holy Gospel according to Mark

Then his mother and his brethren came and sent a
message to him, calling him to them, while they stood
without. There was a multitude sitting round him
when they told him, Here are thy mother and thy
brethren without, looking for thee. And he answered
them, Who is a mother, who are brethren, to me?
Then he looked about at those who were sitting
around him, and said, Here are my mother and my
brethren! If anyone does the will of God, he is my
brother, and sister, and mother.

READING III   Expos., chap. X
A reading from Fr. Hugh of Digne's
Exposition of the Rule

Obedience is twofold, namely, imperfect and perfect. Imperfect obedience is that obedience which is
restricted to certain definite limits, as when a professed friar obeys in those things only which are contained in the Rule or in the Statutes which he has
professed to observe. To this kind of obedience every
religious   is   necessarily   obliged.   But   perfect
obedience—so the Saint points out—does not acknowledge any limits, is not hampered by any bound-
aries, and is not satisfied with the narrow interpreta-
tion of the profession. It extends as far as charity and
willingly and gladly embraces everything that is en-

joined. This is that obedience about which the Apostle Peter so clearly writes: "Now that your obedience to charity has purified your souls,"—beautifully distinguishing it from that obedience which is to a certain extent inactive and servile, not quick in charity, but complying only with necessity.

This supposedly perfect law of obedience, the greatest lover of perfection, Blessed Francis, in his fervent spirit introduced; namely, that his friars should obey not only in those things which they had expressly promised the Lord to observe, but also in all things which were not against their conscience and against their Rule; he set only these two limits to obedience. Indeed, contrary to conscience and contrary to the Rule, neither the superiors have the power to command, nor the subjects have the right to obey. Only these special restrictions does he intend to impose on obedience, as he here restrains both the subjects in obeying and the superiors in commanding when he adds the words: "Not enjoining on them anything which could be against their conscience or our Rule."

But a threefold obedience, namely, of necessity, of charity, and of humility—in accordance as it is exercised towards superiors or towards equals or towards inferiors—the Saint recommends in his Rule based on the perfection of the Gospel.

The obedience of necessity, or of the vow, through which obedience is shown towards superiors, is mainly treated in the present chapter; and about this kind of obedience it is written elsewhere: "When the year of probation has been completed, let them be

received into obedience." The model for this kind of
obedience is Christ, who was made obedient to the
Father even unto death, and who says—in the
Gospel—to the same Father: "Not my will, but your
will be done!"

The obedience of charity the Saint inculcates elsewhere in the Rule when he says: "Wheresoever the
friars are and meet one another, let them show that
they are of the same household, and let them securely
manifest their necessity to one another; for if a
mother nourishes and loves her child according to the
flesh, how much more diligently ought man to love
and nourish his spiritual brother!"

It is especially in caring for one another's needs,
that the friars must render obedience to one another.
That they might do this of their own free will, the
Saint admonished them in the Rule—even before
papal approval—"Through the charity of the spirit let
them willingly serve and obey one another." "This is,"
he says, "the true and holy obedience of our Lord
Jesus Christ." This is the true obedience of Christ,
who in the Gospel teaches us, saying: "Give unto
everyone who asks of you," and again, "This is my
command, that you love one another."

To the obedience of humility, by which obedience is
tendered to inferiors, the Saint in the present chapter
invites the superiors, when he reminds them that
they are the ministers and servants of the other friars. He commanded them to show themselves so
familiar with their subjects who have recourse to
them, "that these same subjects may speak and act
with them as masters with their servants, for so it

ought to be," he remarks, "that the ministers be the servants of all the brethren."

That is to say, as servants obey their masters, so the ministers should obey their subjects in all matters in which they can rightly do so. This kind of obedience Christ displayed in the Gospel when he made himself subject to his Mother and to his Foster-father; also when he, the Lord, chose to be baptized by his servant, John the Baptist, to whom he said: "So it becomes us to fulfill all justice," that is, that perfect humility, whereby the greater subjects himself to the lesser.

12

MINISTERS AND SERVANTS
OF THE BROTHERS

READING I   1 Cor. 9:19-27
A Reading from the First Letter of Paul to the
Corinthians

Thus nobody has any claim on me, and yet I have
made myself everybody's slave, to win more souls.
With the Jews I lived like a Jew, to win the Jews;
with those who keep the law, as one who keeps the
law (though the law had no claim on me), to win those
who kept the law; with those who are free of the law,
like one free of the law (not that I disowned all divine
law, but it was the law of Christ that bound me), to
win those who were free of the law. With the scrupulous, I behaved myself like one who is scrupulous, to
win the scrupulous. I have been everything by turns
to everybody, to bring everybody salvation.

All that I do, I do for the sake of the gospel prom-
ises, to win myself a share in them. You know well
enough that when men run in a race, the race is for
all, but the prize for one; run, then, for victory. Every
athlete must keep all his appetites under control; and
he does it to win a crown that fades, whereas ours is
imperishable. So I do not run my course like a man in
doubt of his goal; I do not fight my battle like a man

who wastes his blows on the air. I buffet my own body, and make it my slave; or I, who have preached to others, may myself be rejected as worthless.

READING II   Mt. 20:20-28
A Reading from the Holy Gospel according to
Matthew

Thereupon the mother of the sons of Zebedee brought them to him, falling on her knees to make a request of him. And when he asked her, What is thy will? she said to him, Here are my two sons; grant that in thy kingdom one may take his place on thy right and the other on thy left. But Jesus answered, You do not know what it is you ask. Have you strength to drink of the cup I am to drink of? They said, We have. And he told them, You shall indeed drink of my cup; but a place on my right hand or my left is not mine to give; it is for those for whom my Father has destined it. The ten others were angry with the two brethren when they heard it; but Jesus called them to him, and said, You know that, among the Gentiles, those who bear rule lord it over them, and great men vaunt their power over them; with you it must be otherwise; whoever would be a great man among you, must be your servant, and whoever has a mind to be first among you must be your slave. So it is that the Son of Man did not come to have service done him; he came to serve others, and to give his life as a ransom for the lives of many.

READING III   Cel., II, nos. 184-187
A Reading from the Second Life
by Fr. Thomas of Celano

Near the end of Francis' vocation in the Lord, a
certain brother who was always solicitous for the
things of God and filled with love for the order, made
this request of Francis: "Father, you will pass away
and the family that has followed you will be left
abandoned in this valley of tears. Point out someone,
if you know of anyone in the order, upon whom your
spirit may rest and upon whom the burden of minister
general may be safely placed." St. Francis answered,
accompanying all his words with sighs: "I see no one,
son, who would be capable of being the leader of an
army of so many different men and the shepherd of so
large a flock. But I would like to describe one for you
and fashion one, as the saying goes, with my hand,
one in whom it may be clearly seen what kind of man
the father of this family must be.

"He must be a man of most serious life," he said, "of
great discretion, of praiseworthy reputation. A man
who has no private loves, lest while he shows favor to
the one, he beget scandal in the whole group. A man
to whom zeal for prayer is a close friend; a man who
sets aside certain hours for his soul and certain hours
for the flock committed to him. For the first thing in
the morning he must begin with the holy sacrifice of
the Mass and commend himself and his flock to the
divine protection in a prolonged devotion. After his
prayers," he said, "he should make himself available
to be stormed by all, to give answers to all, to provide

for all with kindness. He must be a man who will not commit the foul sin of showing favoritism, a man in whom the care of the lowly and the simple is no less pronounced than his care for the wise and the greater. A man who, though it be his gift to excel in learning, bears the image of pious simplicity in his actions and fosters virtue. A man who detests money as the chief cause of the corruption of our profession and perfection; one who, as the head of a poor order, should show himself an example for imitation to the rest, does not make wrong use of the pocketbook. For himself a habit and a little book should suffice, and for his brothers it is enough if he has a box of pens and a seal. He should not be a collector of books, nor given to much reading, lest he be taking from his office what he gives to study. He should be a man who consoles the afflicted, since he is the last recourse for the troubled; and if they can find no healing remedies from him, there is danger that the illness of despair may prevail over the sick. He should bend stormy characters to meekness; he should debase himself and relax something of what is his right to gain a soul for Christ. Toward those who take flight from the order let him not shut up the bowels of his mercy, as if they were sheep who had perished, knowing that the temptations that bring a man to such a pass are overpowering temptations.

"I would want him to be honored by all as taking the place of Christ and to be provided with everything that is necessary in all charity. However, he must not take pleasure in honors, nor be pleased by favors more than by injuries. If some time he should need more abundant food because he has grown weak or is exhausted, he should take it not in private but in public, so that others may be spared shame in providing for the weaknesses of their bodies. Above all else it pertains to him to examine the secrets of consciences, to bring out the truth from hidden places, but not to listen to the talkative. He must be, finally, a man who in no way will bring down the strong fabric of justice by his eagerness for retaining honors, but who will consider so great an office a burden rather than a dignity. However, he should not let apathy grow out of excessive kindness, nor a letdown in discipline out of lax indulgence, so that while he is loved by all, he will be none the less feared by those *that work evil.* I would wish, however, that he have companions endowed with goodness of life who will show themselves, just as he does, *in all things an example of good works:* men who are staunch against pleasures, strong against hardships, and so becomingly affable that all who come to them may be received with holy cheerfulness. Behold," he said, "this is what the minister general of the order must be."

The blessed father required all these same qualities in the ministers provincial too, though in the minister general the single ones had to stand out conspicuously. He wished them to be affable to those in lesser stations, and serene with such great kindness that those who had failed in some way might not be afraid to entrust themselves to their good will. He wanted them to be moderate in giving commands and generous in forgiving offenses; he wanted them to be more ready to bear injuries than to return them; he wanted them to be enemies of vices, but healers of the wicked. Finally, he wanted them to be such that their life would be a mirror of discipline to all the rest. Still he wanted them to be treated with all honor and to be loved, because they bear the burden of cares and labors. He said that they are deserving before God of the highest rewards who govern the souls entrusted to them according to śuch a norm and such a law. (*Omnibus,* pp. 508–511.)

13

POVERTY, SPIRITUAL ASPECT

READING I   2 Cor. 6:1-10
A Reading from the Second Letter of Paul to the
Corinthians

And now, to further that work, we entreat you not
to offer God's grace an ineffectual welcome. (I have
answered thy prayer, he says, in a time of pardon, I
have brought thee help in a day of salvation. And here
is the time of pardon; the day of salvation has come
already.) We are careful not to give offence to anybody, lest we should bring discredit on our ministry;
as God's ministers, we must do everything to make
ourselves acceptable. We have to shew great patience,
in times of affliction, of need, of difficulty; under the
lash, in prison, in the midst of tumult; when we are
tired out, sleepless, and fasting. We have to be pure-
minded, enlightened, forgiving and gracious to others; we have to rely on the Holy Spirit, on unaffected
love, on the truth of our message, on the power of God.
To right and to left we must be armed with innocence;
now honoured, now slighted, now traduced, now flat-
tered. They call us deceivers, and we tell the truth;
unknown, and we are fully acknowledged; dying men,
and see, we live; punished, yes, but not doomed to die;
sad men, that rejoice continually; beggars, that bring
riches to many; disinherited, and the world is ours.

READING II   Mt 5:1-12
A Reading from the Holy Gospel according to Matthew

Jesus, when he saw how great was their number,
went up on to the mountain-side; there he sat down,
and his disciples came about him. And he began
speaking to them; this was the teaching he gave.
Blessed are the poor in spirit; the kingdom of heaven
is theirs. Blessed are the patient; they shall inherit
the land. Blessed are those who mourn; they shall be
comforted. Blessed are those who hunger and thirst
for holiness; they shall have their fill. Blessed are the
merciful; they shall obtain mercy. Blessed are the
clean of heart; they shall see God. Blessed are the
peace-makers; they shall be counted the children of
God. Blessed are those who suffer persecution in the
cause of right; the kingdom of heaven is theirs. Blessed are you, when men revile you, and persecute you
and speak all manner of evil against you falsely, because of me. Be glad and light-hearted, for a rich reward awaits you in heaven; so it was they persecuted
the prophets who went before you.

READING III   Sacr. Com., nos. 1-4, 37
A Reading from the Sacrum Commercium

Among all the excellent and excelling virtues that
prepare in man a place and a dwelling for God and
show man the better and easier way of going to God
and of arriving at him, holy poverty stands out above
all the rest by a certain precedence and excels the

glory of the others by its singular grace; for it is indeed the foundation of all other virtues and their guardian, and it rightly stands first both in place and in name among the other evangelical virtues. The other virtues need not fear the pouring down of rain, the coming of floods, and the blowing of winds that threaten destruction, so long as they are solidly established upon this foundation of poverty.

This is indeed as it should be, for the Son of God, *the Lord of hosts* and *the king of glory,* loved this virtue with a special predilection, sought it out, and found it, when he wrought our salvation upon this earth. At the beginning of his preaching he placed this virtue as a light in the hands of those who enter the portal of faith and made it the foundation stone of his house. The other virtues receive the kingdom of heaven only in promise from him; poverty, however, is already invested with it without delay. For, *blessed are the poor in spirit,* he said, *for theirs is the kingdom of heaven.*

Very properly is the kingdom of heaven said to be the possession of those who keep nothing of the goods of this world through their own will, their inclination toward spiritual things, and their desire for eternal things. For it can only follow that a person will live on heavenly things if he cares nothing for earthly things; and he who renounces all earthly things and *counts them as dung* will taste with pleasure the savory *crumbs that fall from the table* of the holy angels and will deserve to taste how *sweet* and how good the Lord is. This is a true investing with the kingdom of heaven, a security toward the possession of that kingdom, and a kind of foretaste of future happiness.

For this reason Blessed Francis, as a true imitator and disciple of the Savior, gave himself at the beginning of his conversion with all zeal, with all desire and deliberation, to seeking out, finding, and making his own this holy poverty; and in so doing he neither hesitated in adversity, not feared any evil, nor shunned any labor, nor fled from any bodily ills, for he would be satisfied only if his desire to come to poverty, to which the Lord gave *the keys of the kingdom of heaven,* would be granted to him.

Indeed, with the lapse of time, some began to breathe again and to walk again by their own will along the proper way, the way along which some had walked earlier, compelled by necessity. They were men of virtue, men of peace, *blameless in holiness before God our Father,* persisting in *fraternal love* so long as they lived in the flesh, poor in spirit, possessing nothing, rich in holiness of life, abounding in the gifts of the heavenly charismata, *fervent in spirit, rejoicing in hope, patient in tribulation, meek and humble of heart,* preserving peace of spirit, concord of life, harmony of soul, and a cheerful unity in their associations with one another. Finally, these men were devoted to God, pleasing to the angels, beloved of men, strict with themselves, gentle toward others, devout in deed, modest in walk, cheerful of countenance, earnest of heart, humble in prosperity, magnanimous in adversity, temperate at table, most simple in dress, very sparing in sleep, modest and reserved, and conspicuous by the splendor of their good deeds. (*Omnibus,* pp. 1549-1551 and 1572-1573.)

14

POVERTY, ECONOMIC-MATERIAL ASPECT

READING I   2 Cor 8:1-15
A Reading from the Second Letter of Paul to the
Corinthians

And now, brethren, we must tell you about the
grace which God has lavished upon the churches of
Macedonia: how well they have stood the test of distress, how abundantly they have rejoiced over it, how
abject is their poverty, and how the crown of all this
has been a rich measure of generosity in them. I can
testify that of their own accord they undertook to do
all they could, and more than they could; they begged
us, most urgently, to allow them the privilege of help-
ing to supply the needs of the saints. And their gift
went beyond our hopes; they gave their own services
to the Lord, which meant, as God willed, to us; so that
we were able to ask Titus to visit you again, and
finish this gracious task he had begun, as part of his
mission. You excel in so much already, in faith, in
power of utterance, in knowledge of truth, in devotion
of every kind, in your loving treatment of us; may this
gracious excellence be yours too. I say this, not to lay
any injunction on you, but only to make sure that
your charity rings true by telling you about the eagerness of others. (You do not need to be reminded

how gracious our Lord Jesus Christ was; how he impoverished himself for your sakes, when he was so rich, so that you might become rich through his poverty), I am only giving you my advice, then, in this matter; you can claim that as your due, since it was you who led the way, not only in acting, but in proposing to act, as early as last year. It remains for you now to complete your action; readiness of the will must be completed by deeds, as far as your means allow. We value a man's readiness of will according to the means he has, not according to the means he might have, but has not; and there is no intention that others should be relieved at the price of your distress. No, a balance is to be struck, and what you can spare now is to make up for what they want; so that what they can spare may, in its turn, make up for your want, and thus the balance will be redressed. So we read in scripture, He who had gathered much had nothing left over, and he who had gathered little, no lack.

READING II   Lk 18:18-30
A Reading from the Holy Gospel according to Luke

And one of the rulers asked him, Master, who art so good, what must I do to win eternal life? Jesus said to him, Why dost thou call me good? None is good, except God only. Thou knowest the commandments, Thou shalt do no murder, Thou shalt not commit adultery, Thou shalt not steal, Thou shalt not bear false witness, Honour thy father and thy mother. I have kept all these, he said, ever since I grew up. When he heard that, Jesus said, In one thing thou art still wanting; sell all that belongs to thee, and give to the poor; so the treasure thou hast shall be in heaven; then come back and follow me. The answer filled him with sadness, for he was very rich; and Jesus, seeing his mournful look, said, With what difficulty will those who have riches enter God's kingdom! It is easier for a camel to pass through a needle's eye, than for a man to enter the kingdom of God when he is rich. But when he was asked by those who were listening to him, Why then, who can be saved? he told them, What is impossible to man's powers is possible to God.

Hereupon Peter said, And what of us? we have forsaken all that was ours, and followed thee. Jesus said to them, I promise you, everyone who has forsaken home, or parents, or brethren, or wife, or children for the sake of the kingdom of God, will receive, in this present world, many times their worth, and in the world to come, everlasting life.

READING III   Sacr. Com., nos. 59-63
A Reading from the Sacrum Commercium

When everything was ready, the brothers constrained Lady Poverty to eat with them.

But she said: "Show me first your oratory, chapter room, and cloister; your refectory, your kitchen, your dormitory and stable; show me your fine chairs, your polished tables, your great houses. I do not see any of these things. I see only that you are cheerful and happy, overflowing with joy, replete with consolation, as though you expect everything will be given to you just at your wish."

They answered, saying: "Our Lady and our Queen, we, your servants, are tired from our long journey, and you too, coming with us, have suffered not a little. Let us therefore first eat, if it please you, and thus refreshed we will fulfill all your wishes."

"What you say pleases me," she replied; "but now bring water so that we may wash our hands, and towels to dry them."

They very quickly brought a broken earthenware bowl filled with water, for there was not a whole one in that place. And pouring the water over her hands, they looked here and there for a towel. But when they did not find one, one of the brothers gave her the tunic with which he was clothed so that she could dry her hands with it. Taking it with thanks, she magnified God in her heart because he had placed her in the midst of such men.

They then took her to the place where the table was prepared. When she had come there, she looked about, and, seeing nothing but three or four crusts of barley or bran bread placed upon the grass, she was greatly astonished and said to herself: "Who has ever seen such things in the ancient generations? Blessed are you, Lord God, whose is the care of all things; *for* your *power is at hand when* you will; by such works you have *taught your people* to be pleasing to you. They sat down and together they gave thanks to God for all his gifts.

Lady Poverty then commanded the cooked food to be brought in dishes. And behold, a single dish was brought filled with cold water, that they might all dip their bread in it; there was neither an abundance of dishes there nor a variety of cooked foods.

She asked that she be given at least some uncooked, sweet-smelling herbs. But since they had no gardener and knew nothing of a garden, they gathered some wild herbs in the woods and set these before her.

She said: "Bring me a little salt to season the herbs, for they are bitter."

And they said: "Wait, Lady, and we will go to the city and get some for you, if some one will give it to us."

"Well, then," she said, "give me a knife so I may cut off what is superfluous and that I may cut the bread, which is very hard and dry."

"Lady," they said to her, "we have no blacksmith to make swords for us. For now, just use your teeth in place of a knife and later we will get one for you."

"And do you have a little wine?" she asked.

But they answered and said: "Lady, we do not have any wine, *for the chief thing for man's life is water and bread,* and it is not good for you to drink wine, for the spouse of Christ must shun wine like poison."

But after they had been more satisfied from the glory of such great want than they would have been from an abundance of all things, they blessed the Lord in whose eyes they had found such grace; and they led Lady Poverty to the place where she might rest since she was tired. There she lay down in her total nothingness upon the bare ground.

She also begged a cushion for her head. Immediately they brought a stone and placed it under her head.

She, indeed, slept a most peaceful and sober sleep. Then she quickly arose and asked to be shown the cloister. Taking her to a certain hill, they showed her the whole world, as far as she could see, and said: "This, Lady, is our cloister." (*Omnibus,* pp. 1591–1593.)

15

CHASTITY
FOR THE SAKE OF GOD'S KINGDOM

READING I   1 Cor. 7:32-35
A Reading from the First Letter of Paul to the
Corinthians

And I would have you free from concern. He who is
unmarried is concerned with God's claim, asking how
he is to please God; whereas the married man is concerned with the world's claim, asking how he is to
please his wife; and thus he is at issue with himself.
So a woman who is free of wedlock, or a virgin, is
concerned with the Lord's claim, intent on holiness,
bodily and spiritual; whereas the married woman is
concerned with the world's claim, asking how she is to
please her husband.

I am thinking of your own interest when I say this.
It is not that I would hold you in a leash; I am thinking of what is suitable for you, and how you may best
attend on the Lord without distraction.

READING II   Mt 19:3-12
A Reading from the Holy Gospel according to
Matthew

He told them, It was to suit your hard hearts that
Moses allowed you to put your wives away; it was not
so at the beginning of things. And I tell you that he

who puts away his wife, not for any unfaithfulness of hers, and so marries another, commits adultery; and he too commits adultery, who marries her after she has been put away. At this, his disciples said to him, If the case stands so between man and wife, it is better not to marry at all. That conclusion, he said, cannot be taken in by everybody, but only by those who have the gift. There are some eunuchs, who were so born from the mother's womb, some were made so by men, and some have made themselves so for love of the kingdom of heaven; take this in, you whose hearts are large enough for it.

READING III   Leg. Major, chap. V, 3-5
A Reading from the Major Life by St. Bonaventure

Francis watched over himself with rigid self-discipline and was especially careful to preserve perfect purity of soul and body.

One night when he was praying in his cell at the hermitage of Sarteano, the Devil called him three times, "Francis, Francis, Francis." When Francis replied, asking him what he wanted, the Devil went on, "There is not a sinner in the whole world whom God will not forgive, if he repents. But if a man kills himself by doing too much penance, he will never find forgiveness." By God's inspiration the saint saw his treachery at once and realized that Satan was trying to reduce him to half-heartedness. This was proved by what followed, because he immediately felt a grave

temptation of the flesh, provoked by him whose "very
breath will set coals aflame" (Jb 41, 12). The moment
he felt it coming, Francis tore off his habit in his love
for chastity and began to scourge himself with a cord.
"There, brother ass," he exclaimed, "that is your
place, to be scourged like that. The habit is a sign of
the religious state and an indication of a good life; a
lustful person has no right to it. If you want to go
another road, off with you!" Then in an excess of
fervor he opened the door and went out into the garden where he rolled naked in the deep snow. After
that he gathered up some of it with both hands and
made seven heaps with it and stood before them, saying to his body, "Look, the big one here is your wife
and those four are your children, two boys and two
girls. The other two are the servants you need to look
after them, a man and a woman. And now hurry up
and find clothes for them—they are dying of cold. But
if all the trouble it takes to look after them is too
much for you, then keep your services for God alone."
At that the tempter took his leave defeated, and the
saint returned triumphantly to his cell. The cold had
pierced him to the bone but the flame of passion
within him had been utterly quenched, so that he
never felt anything like it again. A friar who had
been busy praying at the time saw what happened in
the clear moonlight. When Francis discovered that he
had been seen, he told him all about the temptation
which he had felt and commanded him never to tell
anyone what he had seen during his lifetime.

Besides teaching the friars to mortify the passions
of the flesh with its impulses, Francis insisted that

they should watch over their exterior senses, by
which death enters the soul, with the greatest
vigilance. He warned them to beware of the sight of
women and avoid close friendships or conversation
with them which can often lead to a fall. Indiscretion
in this matter, he affirmed, could crush the weak and
weaken the strong, adding that it was as hard for
anyone who had much to do with them to avoid being
ensnared as it was to "walk on hot coals without burning one's feet" (cf. Prv 6, 27). He avoided the sight of
women so carefully himself that he scarcely knew any
woman by sight, as he once confessed to his companion. He was convinced that it was dangerous to allow
any representation of them to enter one's mind because the flames of passion could easily be rekindled
or the purity of a clean heart be stained. He often
remarked that any conversation with women was
pointless except on the occasion of confession or a
brief instruction. Such contact could be of benefit to
their spiritual progress and did not exceed the limits
of religious behavior. "What," he asked, "has a religious got to do with women anyway, unless they are
looking for confession or ask for spiritual direction?
When a man is too sure of himself, he becomes less
wary of the enemy, and if the Devil can call his own
even one hair of a man's head, he will lose no time in
making a rope of it." (*Omnibus,* pp. 664–666.)

16

**CHASTITY
NO SUSPICIOUS RELATIONSHIPS**

READING I   1 Cor 6:12-17, 19-20
A Reading from the First Letter of Paul to the
Corinthians

I am free to do what I will; yes, but not everything
can be done without harm. I am free to do what I will,
but I must not abdicate my own liberty. Food is meant
for our animal nature, and our animal nature claims
its food; true enough, but then, God will bring both
one and the other to an end. But your bodies are not
meant for debauchery, they are meant for the Lord,
and the Lord claims your bodies. And God, just as he
has raised our Lord from the dead, by his great power
will raise us up too. Have you never been told that
your bodies belong to the body of Christ? And am I to
take what belongs to Christ and make it one with a
harlot? God forbid. Or did you never hear that the
man who unites himself to a harlot becomes one body
with her? The two, we are told, will become one flesh.
Whereas the man who unites himself to the Lord becomes one spirit with him.

Surely you know that your bodies are the shrines of
the Holy Spirit, who dwells in you. And he is God's
gift to you, so that you are no longer your own masters. A great price was paid to ransom you; glorify
God by making your bodies the shrines of his presence.

READING II   Mt 5:27-29
A Reading from the Holy Gospel according to
Matthew

You have heard that it was said, Thou shalt not
commit adultery. But I tell you that he who casts his
eyes on a woman so as to lust after her has already
committed adultery with her in his heart. If thy right
eye is the occasion of·thy falling into sin, pluck it out
and cast it away from thee: better to lose one part of
thy body than to have the whole cast into hell.

READING III   Cel. II, nos. 112-114
A Reading from the Second Life
by Fr. Thomas of Celano

That honeyed poison, namely, familiarities with
women, which lead astray even holy men, Francis
commanded should be entirely avoided. For he feared
that from such things the weak spirit would be
quickly broken and the strong spirit often weakened.

Francis was accustomed to combat unclean eyes
with the following parable: "A very powerful king
sent two messengers to the queen one after the other.
The first came back and reported only her words in
exact words. For *the eyes of a wise man are in his
head,* and he did not let them roam about. The other
returned and after a few short words about her message, he recounted a long story of the lady's beauty.
'Truly, lord,' he said, 'I have seen a most beautiful

woman. Happy he that enjoys her.' But the king said: 'Wicked servant, you have cast impure eyes upon my wife? It is evident that you wished to purchase what you looked upon so sharply.' He commanded that the first messenger be called back and said to him:'What do you think of the queen?' And he said: 'I think very well of her, for she listened silently and replied wisely.' 'And there is no beauty in her?' the king said. 'It is for you, my lord,' he said, 'to look upon that; my business was only to deliver a message.' Then this sentence was pronounced by the king: 'You,' he said, 'are chaste of eye, and being even more chaste of body, you shall be my chamberlain. But let this other man depart from my house lest he defile my marriage bed.' "

Once it happened, when St. Francis was going to Bevagna, that he was not able to reach the town because of his weakness from fasting. His companion, however, sending a messenger to a certain spiritual woman, humbly begged bread and wine for the saint. When she heard this, she ran to the saint along with her daughter, a virgin vowed to God, carrying what was necessary. But after the saint had been refreshed and somewhat strengthened, he in turn refreshed the mother and her daughter with the word of God. But while he preached to them, he did not look either of them in the face. When they departed his companion said to Francis: "Why, Brother, did you not look at the holy virgin who came with such great devotion?" The father answered: "Who must not fear to look upon the bride of Christ? But when a sermon is preached with the eyes and the face she looks at me, but not I at her." (*Omnibus,* pp. 454–457.)

17

MINORITES
HUMILITY, TRUE GLORY

READING I   Phil 2:1-7
A Reading from the Letter of Paul to the Philippians

If anything is meant by encouragement in Christ, by loving sympathy, by common fellowship in the spirit, by feelings of tenderness and pity, fill up my cup of happiness by thinking with the same mind, cherishing the same bond of charity, soul knit to soul in a common unity of thought. You must never act in a spirit of factiousness, or of ambition; each of you must have the humility to think others better men than himself, and study the welfare of others, not his own. Yours is to be the same mind which Christ Jesus shewed. His nature is, from the first, divine, and yet he did not see, in the rank of Godhead, a prize to be coveted; he dispossessed himself, and took the nature of a slave, fashioned in the likeness of men, and presenting himself to us in human form.

READING II   Lk 14:7-14
A Reading from the Holy Gospel according to Luke

He also had a parable for the guests who were invited, as he observed how they chose the chief places
for themselves; he said to them: When any man invites thee to a wedding, do not sit down in the chief
place; he may have invited some guest whose rank is
greater than thine. If so, his host and thine will come
and say to thee, Make room for this man; and so thou
wilt find thyself taking, with a blush, the lowest place
of all. Rather, when thou art summoned, go straight
to the lowest place and sit down there; so, when he
who invited thee comes in, he will say, My friend, go
higher than this; and then honour shall be thine before all that sit down in thy company. Everyone who
exalts himself shall be humbled, and he that humbles
himself shall be exalted. He said, moreover, to his
host, When thou givest a dinner or a supper, do not
ask thy neighbours to come, or thy brethren, or thy
kindred, or thy friends who are rich; it may be they
will send thee invitations in return, and so thou wilt
be recompensed for thy pains. Rather, when thou
givest hospitality, invite poor men to come, the crip-
ples, the lame, the blind: so thou shalt win a blessing,
for these cannot make thee any return; thy reward
will come when the just rise again.

A Reading from Fr. Hugh of Digne's
Exposition of the Rule

The most holy Founder of our Rule, very earnestly
desiring to follow the footsteps of Christ in his Gospel
way of life, based his religious profession on the ob-
servance of the Gospel. Even the name of Friars
Minor is borrowed from the Gospel, where the Lord
says: "As long as you did it for one of these, the least
of my brethren, you did it for me," and a little later on
"As long as you did not do it for one of these least
ones, you did not do it for me."

Through this name, the Saint expressed not only
the poverty, but also that exceptional lowliness in
which he wished his friars to live, so that not only in
name but also in their conduct they might be the most
lowly. This lowliness is such an integral part of the
life of a Friar Minor, that through his name, through
his dress, through every aspect of his life it is recommended in the Rule; so that whoever refuses to be
lowly, certainly cannot be a Friar Minor.

It is the hall-mark of a Friar Minor to embrace
lowliness and to shun every exalted position; eagerly
to avoid every prominence in word or action or behavior or conversation; never to parade before men as
superior to any others, whether religious or lay-
persons. Comparisons are odious and can scarely ever
be made without giving scandal or betraying a brag-
ging disposition. It is characteristic of a Friar Minor
that—in accordance with his name—he strive to what
is lowly, and it is becoming that he feel his own lowli-

ness and show due reverence to all others as is proper. In this way the early friars acted, being subject to every human creature out of love for God.

Lowliness—which is pleasing to God and to men— should necessarily be the most distinctive and special virtue of the Friars Minor, as is demanded by their very name and their state as lowly persons. An enduring patience and a universal charity which lovingly embraces even those who persecute us,—these are the manners and the ideals which we should most earnestly strive to acquire. Genuine lowliness, charity, and patience prove more than anything else the genuine quality of this state of life.

If we wholeheartedly embrace lowliness and charity, if we in a gentle heart preserve an unwearied patience towards those who heap injuries and insults and calumnies upon us—even while we are kind to them—and in no way return evil for evil either by deed or word or the least sign of anger—which should not in any way be manifested in religious persons— but rather (as we are instructed in the Gospel) repay them with our prayers and our kind deeds, thereby we prove that we are genuine Friars Minor. These acts of ours either clearly betray the defect in our Gospel profession or they prove its perfection in us.

18

FRATERNITY

READING I   1 Pt 4:7-11
A Reading from the First Letter of Peter

The end of all things is close at hand; live wisely, and keep your senses awake to greet the hours of prayer. Above all things, preserve constant charity among yourselves; charity draws the veil over a multitude of sins. Make one another free of what is yours ungrudgingly, sharing with all whatever gift each of you has received, as befits the stewards of a God so rich in graces. One of you preaches, let him remember that it is God's message he is uttering; another distributes relief, let him remember that it is God who supplies him the opportunity; that so, in all you do, God may be glorified through Jesus Christ; to him be the glory and the power through endless ages, Amen.

READING II   Jn 15:9-17
A Reading from the Holy Gospel according to John

I have bestowed my love upon you, just as my Father has bestowed his love upon me; live on, then, in my love. You will live on in my love, if you keep my commandments, just as it is by keeping my Father's commandments that I live on in his love.

All this I have told you, so that my joy may be yours, and the measure of your joy may be filled up. This is my commandment, that you should love one another, as I have loved you. This is the greatest love a man can shew, that he should lay down his life for his friends; and you, if you do all that I command you, are my friends. I do not speak of you any more as my servants; a servant is one who does not understand what his master is about, whereas I have made known to you all that my Father has told me; and so I have called you my friends. It was not you that chose me, it was I that chose you. The task I have appointed you is to go out and bear fruit, fruit which will endure; so that every request you make of the Father in my name may be granted you. These are the directions I give you, that you should love one another.

READING III   Expos., chap. VI
A Reading from Fr. Hugh of Digne's
Exposition of the Rule

"Wheresoever the brethren are and meet one another, let them show that they are of one household, and let them securely manifest their necessity to one another; for if a mother nourishes and loves her child according to the flesh, how much more diligently ought man to love and nourish his spiritual Brother!" By these words it is clearly demonstrated how perfect the charity must be among the friars; namely, in its manifestation, in its intensity, and in deed.

With regard to the manifestation of charity, it is said: "Let them show that they are of one household, and let them securely manifest their necessity to one another." It does not suffice for a Friar Minor to refrain from hating his brother; for that much is demanded of every Christian, however imperfect. But every friar owes to his confreres such an external show of familiarity and such signs of family love, that one may manifest his necessity to another as he would to a member of the same family. Thus the Saint in his earlier Rule said: "Let each one securely manifest to another his necessity, in order that he might obtain the necessary help and service." Again he says: "Wheresoever the brethren dwell, let them frequently visit one another and show respect to one another without murmuring. And let them take care not to appear sad and gloomy like hypocrites, but let them be joyful and contented in the Lord, and becomingly courteous."

How great should be the intensity of love is described by the example of a mother who is most strongly drawn to her child, when he adds: "For if a mother nourishes and loves her child according to the flesh, how much more diligently ought man to love and nourish his spiritual brother!" Concerning the intensity of charity, the words are added: "And if one of them should fall sick, the other brethren must serve him as they would wish to be served themselves." The friars are bound to serve each other as they themselves would wish to be served,—with due regard to our state of life and to the nature of the sickness and of the person. Charity proves itself in time of need: Nothing proves friendship better than the carrying of a friend's burden.

The friars are obliged—according to their ability—to render faithful service to the needs of their confreres in the same way they themselves would desire to be served. Acting otherwise, they would not only sin against the Rule, but also harm themselves. For if anyone denies to his confrere the needed help, he by his bad example induces others to deny him the same kind of help when he needs it. And so, little by little, charity will grow cold, if it is not exercised in time of need.

The above-mentioned charity was most fervent among the early friars. Offering themselves and all they had with a wonderful mutual readiness, they cared not only for those who lived with them, but also for all strangers that came along. For the friars received all guests—whether known or unknown—as if they were angels from God, and they did this with the greatest possible charity. As soon as their guests arrived, they hastened to wash their feet and hurriedly prepared whatever was needed by the weary pilgrims. They did not look upon them as strangers, but considered them their brothers, and in a true family spirit generously offered them food and all other necessities, as if they were members of the same household. And in their works of charity and mercy, which they had to exercise, there was no false show or fraud, but all was hidden under the cover of genuine love.

So I have sometimes seen in solitary places friars in extreme poverty caring for the sick and the feeble with such charity as we had never seen elsewhere, and—according to the Rule—acting towards them as most solicitous mothers. They were austere and indigent for themselves, but they knew no bounds in caring for the needs of others.

Charity does not know how to hide what it has, but freely shares everything, offering advice and intent on giving assistance, and not withholding any aid from a needy brother. Selfish love impedes such universal charity. For those who love themselves and are inordinately attached to the goods they use, do not subject their body to labor nor as freely dispose of their goods for their brothers, as charity demands. But the true servants of God steadfastly cling to charity and strive to promote it in themselves and in others, because that constitutes the fulfillment of the law. In this Order, that kind of charity is said to hold top priority even to the present day.

19

TRANSITUS
SISTER DEATH

READING I   Phil 1:19-26
A Reading from the Letter of Paul to the Philippians

I am well assured that this will make for my soul's health, with you to pray for me, and Jesus Christ to supply my needs with his Spirit. This is my earnest longing and my hope, that I shall never be put to the blush; that I shall speak with entire freedom, and so this body of mine will do Christ honour, now as always, in life or in death. For me, life means Christ; death is a prize to be won. But what if living on in this mortal body is the only way to harvest what I have sown? Thus I cannot tell what to choose; I am hemmed in on both sides. I long to have done with it, and be with Christ, a better thing, much more than a better thing; and yet, for your sakes, that I should wait in the body is more urgent still. I am certain of that, and I do not doubt that I shall wait, and wait upon you all, to the happy furtherance of your faith. Yes, you shall be prouder of me than ever in Christ Jesus, when I come once again to visit you.

READING II Jn 12:20-33
A Reading from the Holy Gospel according to John

And there were certain Gentiles, among those that had come up to worship at the feast, who approached Philip, the man from Bethsaida in Galilee, and made a request of him; Sir, they said, we desire to see Jesus. Philip came and told Andrew, and together Andrew and Philip went and told Jesus. And Jesus answered them thus, The time has come now for the Son of Man to achieve his glory. Believe me when I tell you this; a grain of wheat must fall into the ground and die, or else it remains nothing more than a grain of wheat; but if it dies, then it yields rich fruit. He who loves his life will lose it; he who is an enemy to his own life in this world will keep it, so as to live eternally. If anyone is to be my servant, he must follow my way; so shall my servant too be where I am. If anyone serves me, my Father will do him honour.

And now my soul is distressed. What am I to say? I will say, Father, save me from undergoing this hour of trial; and yet, I have only reached this hour of trial that I might undergo it. Father, make thy name known. And at this, a voice came from heaven, I have made it known, and will yet make it known. Thereupon the multitude which stood listening declared that it had thundered; but some of them said, An angel has spoken to him. Jesus answered, It was for your sake, not for mine, that this utterance was made. Sentence is now being passed on this world; now is the time when the prince of this world is to be cast out. Yes, if only I am lifted up from the earth, I will attract

all men to myself. (In saying this, he prophesied the
death he was to die.)

Cel. II, nos., 216-217
A Reading from the Second Life
by Thomas of Celano

After these things, the saint raised his hands to
heaven and praised his Christ, because, freed now of
all things, he was going to him free. Indeed, that he
might show himself to be a true imitator of Christ his
God in all things, he *loved to the end* his brothers and
sons whom he had loved from the beginning. He had
all the brothers present there called to him and sooth-
ing them with comforting words in view of his death,
he exhorted them with paternal affection to love God.
He spoke a long time about practicing patience and
poverty, setting the counsels of the holy Gospel ahead
of all other prescriptions. Then, with all the brothers
sitting about, he extended his right hand over them
and beginning with his vicar, he placed it upon the
head of each one. "Farewell," he said, "all you my
sons, *in the fear of the Lord,* and may you remain in
him always! And because a future temptation and
tribulation is approaching, happy will they be who
will persevere in the things they have begun. I am
hastening to the Lord, to whose grace I commend you
all." And he blessed in those who were present also all
his brothers in the world and all who would come
after them unto the end of the world.

While therefore the brothers were weeping very

bitterly and grieving inconsolably, the holy father commanded that bread be brought to him. He *blessed and broke it* and gave a small piece of it to each one to eat. Commanding also that a book of the Gospels be brought, he asked that the Gospel according to St. John be read to him from the place that begins: *Before the feast of the Passover.* He was recalling that most holy supper which the Lord celebrated as his last supper with his disciples. He did all of this in reverent memory of that supper, showing thereby the deep love he had for his brothers.

Then he spent the few days that remained before his death in praise, teaching his companions whom he loved so much to praise Christ with him. He himself, in as far as he was able, broke forth in this psalm: *I cried to the Lord with my voice: with my voice I made supplication to the Lord.* He also invited all creatures to praise God, and by means of the words he had composed earlier, he exhorted them to love God. He exhorted death itself, terrible and hateful to all, to give praise, and going joyfully to meet it, he invited it to make its lodging with him. "Welcome," he said, "my sister death." To the doctor he said: "Tell me bravely, brother doctor, that death, which is the gateway of life, is at hand." Then to the brothers: "When you see that I am brought to my last moments, place me naked upon the ground just as you saw me the day before yesterday; and let me lie there after I am dead for the length of time it takes one to walk a mile unhurriedly." The hour therefore came, and all the mysteries of Christ being fulfilled in him, he winged his way happily to God. (*Omnibus,* pp. 535-536.)

20

THE POVERELLO

READING I   Gal 6:14-18
A Reading from the Letter of Paul to the Galatians

God forbid that I should make a display of anything, except the cross of our Lord Jesus Christ,
through which the world stands crucified to me, and I
to the world. Circumcision means nothing, the want
of it means nothing; when a man is in Christ Jesus,
there has been a new creation. Peace and pardon to
all those who follow this rule, to God's true Israel.
Spare me, all of you, any further anxieties; already I
bear the scars of the Lord Jesus printed on my body.
Brethren, the grace of our Lord Jesus Christ be with
your spirit. Amen.

READING II   Mt 11:25-30
A Reading from the Holy Gospel according to
Matthew

At that time Jesus said openly, Father, who art
Lord of heaven and earth, I give thee praise that thou
hast hidden all this from the wise and the prudent,

and revealed it to little children. Be it so, Father, since this finds favour in thy sight. My Father has entrusted everything into my hands; none knows the Son truly except the Father, and none knows the Father truly except the Son, and those to whom it is the Son's good pleasure to reveal him.

Come to me, all you that labour and are burdened; I will give you rest. Take my yoke upon yourselves, and learn from me; I am gentle and humble of heart; and you shall find rest for your souls. For my yoke is easy, and my burden is light.

READING III   Leg. Major, Prologus, 1-2
A Reading from the Major Life by St. Bonaventure

In these last times the grace of God our Savior has dawned in his servant Francis on all who are truly humble and love poverty. In him we can contemplate the excess of God's mercy and his example urges us to forego completely irreverent thoughts and worldly appetites and live like Christ, looking forward eagerly to the happiness that is our hope. He was despised and humbled, but the Most High looked upon him with such condescension and kindness that he was not content merely to raise him from the dust and choose him out from the world, but he inspired him to profess the life of Gospel perfection and made him a leader and an apostle. He was to be a light for those who believe that, by bearing witness of the light, he might prepare a way for the Lord to the hearts of his faithful, a way of light and peace. By the glorious splendor of his life and teaching Francis shone like the day-star amid the clouds, and by the brilliance which radiated from him he guided those who live in darkness, in the shadow of death, to the light. Like the rainbow that lights up the clouds with sudden glory (Sir 50, 8), he bore in his own body the pledge of God's covenant, bringing the good news of peace and salvation to men, like a true Angel of peace. Like St. John the Baptist, he was appointed by God to prepare a way in the desert—that is, by the complete renunciation involved in perfect poverty—and preach repentance by word and example.

God forestalled him by the gift of his divine grace, so that he won the praise of heroic virtue. Then he was filled with the spirit of prophecy and charged with the ministry of Angels, as he burned with the flames of a love worthy of the Seraphim. Like a man who has joined the ranks of the Angels, he was taken up in a chariot of fire, so that there can be no doubt whatever that he came "in the spirit and power of an Elias" (Lk 1, 17), as we shall see in the course of his life. Therefore there is every reason to believe that it is he who is referred to under the image of an Angel coming up from the east, with the seal of the living God, in the prophecy made by another friend of Christ the Bridegroom, St. John the Apostle and Evangelist. When the sixth seal was broken, St. John tells us in the Apocalypse, "I saw a second Angel coming up from the east, with the seal of the living God" (Ap 7, 12).

If we consider the perfection of his extraordinary

sanctity, we can see beyond all shadow of doubt that this messenger of God was his servant Francis who was found worthy to be loved by Christ, imitated by us, and admired by the whole world. Even while he lived on earth among human beings, he shared the sinlessness of the Angels, so that he became an example to those who followed Christ perfectly. We have plenty of reason to be firmly convinced of this. First of all, there is the mission which he had received "to summon all men to mourn and lament, to shave their heads and wear sackcloth" (Is 22, 12) "and mark the brows of those that weep and wail with a cross" (Ez 9, 4), signing them with the cross of penance and clothing them in his own habit which was shaped like a cross. But besides that, we have an unimpeachable testimony, the seal of truth itself which was impressed on his body and which made him like the living God, Christ crucified. This was not the work of nature's powers or of any human agent, it was accomplished by the miraculous power of the Spirit of the living God alone. (*Omnibus,* pp. 631-632.)

21

CANTICLE OF THE CREATURES

Sir 39:16, 18-32, 37-41
A Reading from the Book of Sirach

And still I have thoughts worth the telling; madman as easily might contain himself.

Yours to yield the frangrance of incense; yours to blossom like the lily, and smell sweet, and put forth leaves for your adornment; yours to sing songs of praise, and bless the Lord for all things he has made. His name extol; songs of praise let your lips utter, and let harp's melody mingle with the song. And you shall praise him in these words following.

Good, wondrously good, is all the Lord has made. Piled high the waters stand at his command, shut in by cisterns of his appointing. All-sufficient is his will, unfailing his power to save; open to his view are all deeds of mortal men, nothing can escape that scrutiny. On every age of time his glance rests; marvel is none beyond his compass. Not for man to ask what this or that may be, each shall be needed in its turn. His blessings flow like a stream in full flood, like rain pouring down to refresh the parched earth. But the nations that never look to find him, shall be the prey of his vengeance; did he not turn the waters into firm ground, and dry up the floor of them, so that it made a path for the passage of his own people, and yet a trap to punish the wicked?

From the first, good things were made for good men to enjoy; for sinners, they are good and evil at once. What are the first needs of man's life? Water, fire, iron, salt, milk, wheat-meal, honey, the grape-cluster, oil and clothing. Thereby, for just men, nought but good is intended, yet for sinners they turn to evil.

All these hold high revel as they perform his will; ready they stand till earth has need of them, and when the need comes, they will obey.

From the first, all my questioning and all my thought confirms me in what I have written, all things God has made are good, and each of them serves its turn; nor ever must we complain things have happened for the worse, since each has its own occasion to justify it. With full hearts, then, and full voice, praise we and bless the Lord's name.

READING II   Mt 6:19-34
A Reading from the Holy Gospel according to
Matthew

Do not lay up treasure for yourselves on earth, where there is moth and rust to consume it, where there are thieves to break in and steal it; lay up treasure for yourselves in heaven, where there is no moth or rust to consume it, no thieves to break in and steal. Where your treasure-house is, there your heart is too. The eye is the light of the whole body, so that if thy eye is clear, the whole of thy body will be lit up;

whereas if thy eye is diseased, the whole of thy body will be in darkness. And if the light which thou hast in thee is itself darkness, what of thy darkness? How deep will that be! A man cannot be the slave of two masters at once; either he will hate the one and love the other, or he will devote himself to the one and despise the other. You must serve God or money; you cannot serve both.

I say to you, then, do not fret over your life, how to support it with food and drink; over your body, how to keep it clothed. Is not life itself a greater gift than food, the body than clothing? See how the birds of the air never sow, or reap, or gather grain into barns, and yet your heavenly Father feeds them; have you not an excellence beyond theirs? Can any one of you, for all his anxiety, add a cubit's growth to his height? And why should you be anxious over clothing? See how the wild lilies grow; they do not toil or spin; and yet I tell you that even Solomon in all his glory was not ar-rayed like one of these. If God, then, so clothes the grasses of the field, which to-day live and will feed the oven to-morrow, will he not be much more ready to clothe you, men of little faith? Do not fret, then, ask-ing, What are we to eat? or What are we to drink? or How shall we find clothing? It is for the heathen to busy themselves over such things; you have a Father in heaven who knows that you need them all. Make it your first care to find the kingdom of God, and his approval, and all these things shall be yours without the asking. Do not fret, then, over to-morrow; leave to-morrow to fret over its own needs; for to-day, to-day's troubles are enough.

READING III   Cel. I nos. 80-81, II, no. 165
A Reading from the Lives by Fr. Thomas of Celano

It would take too long and it would be impossible to enumerate and gather together all the things the glorious Francis did and taught while he was living in the flesh. For who could ever give expression to the very great affection he bore for all things that are God's? Who would be able to narrate the sweetness he enjoyed while contemplating in creatures the wisdom of their Creator, his power and his goodness? Indeed, he was very often filled with a wonderful and ineffable joy from this consideration while he looked upon the sun, while he beheld the moon, and while he gazed upon the stars and the firmament. O simple piety and pious simplicity!

For as of old the three youths in the fiery furnace invited all the elements to praise and glorify the Creator of the universe, so also this man, filled with the spirit of God, never ceased to glorify, praise, and bless the Creator and Ruler of all things in all the elements and creatures.

How great a gladness do you think the beauty of the flowers brought to his mind when he saw the shape of their beauty and perceived the odor of their sweetness? He used to turn the eye of consideration immediately to the beauty of that flower that comes *from the root of Jesse* and gives light *in the days of spring* and by its fragrance has raised innumerable thousands from the dead.

Hurrying to leave this world in as much as it is the place of exile of our pilgrimage, this blessed traveler was yet helped not a little by the things that are in the world. With respect to the *world-rulers of this darkness,* he used it as a field of battle; with respect to God, he used it as a very bright *image of his goodness.* In every work of the artist he praised the Artist; whatever he found in the things made he referred to the Maker. He rejoiced in all the works of the hands of the Lord and saw behind things pleasant to behold their life-giving reason and cause. In beautiful things he saw Beauty itself; all things were to him good. "He who made us is the best," they cried out to him. Through his footprints impressed upon things he followed the Beloved everywhere; he made for himself from all things a ladder by which *to come even to his throne.*

He embraced all things with a rapture of unheard of devotion, speaking to them of the Lord and admonishing them to praise him. He spared lights, lamps, and candles, not wishing to extinguish their brightness with his hand, for he regarded them as a symbol of Eternal Light. He walked reverently upon stones, because of him who was called the Rock. When he used this versicle: *Thou hast exalted me on a rock,* he would say for the sake of greater reverence: *Thou hast exalted me at the foot of a rock.*

He forbade the brothers to cut down the whole tree when they cut wood, so that it might have hope of sprouting again. He commanded the gardener to leave the border around the garden undug, so that in their proper times the greenness of the grass and the beauty of flowers might announce the beauty of the Father of all things. He commanded that a little place

be set aside in the garden for sweet-smelling and
flowering plants, so that they would bring those who
look upon them to the memory of the Eternal Sweetness.

He removed from the road little worms, lest they be
crushed under foot; and he ordered that honey and the
best wines be set out for the bees, lest they perish
from want in the cold of winter. He called all animals
by the name *brother,* though among all the kinds of
animals he preferred the gentle. Who could possibly
narrate everything? For that original goodness that
will be one day *all things in all* already shown forth in
this saint *all things in all.* (*Omnibus,* pp. 295–296 and
494–495.)

22

DISCRETION
EXAMINE ALL THINGS AND KEEP WHAT IS GOOD

READING I   1 Cor 2:6-16
A Reading from the First Letter of Paul to the
Corinthians

There is, to be sure, a wisdom which we make
known among those who are fully grounded; but it is
not the wisdom of this world, or of this world's rulers,
whose power is to be abrogated. What we make
known is the wisdom of God, his secret, kept hidden
til now; so, before the ages, God had decreed, reserving glory for us. (None of the rulers of this world could
read his secret, or they would not have crucified him
to whom all glory belongs.) So we read of, Things no
eye has seen, no ear has heard, no human heart conceived, the welcome God has prepared for those who
love him. To us, then, God has made a revelation of it
through his Spirit; there is no depth in God's nature
so deep that the Spirit cannot find it out. Who else can
know a man's thoughts, except the man's own spirit
that is within him? So no one else can know God's
thoughts, but the Spirit of God. And what we have
received is no spirit of worldly wisdom; it is the Spirit
that comes from God, to make us understand God's
gifts to us; gifts which we make known, not in such

words as human wisdom teaches, but in words taught us by the Spirit, matching what is spiritual with what is spiritual. Mere man with his natural gifts cannot take in the thoughts of God's Spirit; they seem mere folly to him, and he cannot grasp them, because they demand a scrutiny which is spiritual. Whereas the man who has spiritual gifts can scrutinize everything, without being subject, himself, to any other man's scrutiny. Who has entered into the mind of the Lord, so as to be able to instruct him? And Christ's mind is ours.

READING II   Mt 6:1-18
A Reading from the Holy Gospel according to
Matthew

Be sure you do not perform your acts of piety before men, for them to watch; if you do that, you have no title to a reward from your Father who is in heaven. Thus, when thou givest alms, do not sound a trumpet before thee, as the hypocrites do in synagogues and in streets, to win the esteem of men. Believe me, they have their reward already. But when thou givest alms, thou shalt not so much as let thy left hand know what thy right hand is doing, so secret is thy almsgiving to be; and then thy Father, who sees what is done in secret, will reward thee. And when you pray, you are not to be like hypocrites, who love to stand praying in synagogues or at street-corners, to be a mark for men's eyes; believe me, they have their reward already. But when thou art praying, go into thy inner room and shut the door upon thyself, and so pray to thy Father in secret; and then thy Father, who sees what is done in secret, will reward thee.

Moreover, when you are at prayer, do not use many phrases, like the heathens, who think to make themselves heard by their eloquence. You are not to be like them; your heavenly Father knows well what your needs are before you ask him. This, then, is to be your prayer, Our Father, who art in heaven, hallowed be thy name; thy kingdom come; thy will be done, on earth as it is in heaven; give us this day our daily bread; and forgive us our trespasses, as we forgive them that trespass against us; and lead us not into temptation, but deliver us from evil. Amen. Your heavenly Father will forgive you your transgressions, if you forgive your fellow-men theirs; if you do not forgive them, your heavenly Father will not forgive your transgressions either.

Again, when you fast, do not shew it by gloomy looks, as the hypocrites do. They make their faces unsightly, so that men can see they are fasting; believe me, they have their reward already. But do thou, at thy times of fasting, anoint thy head and wash thy face, so that thy fast may not be known to men, but to thy Father who dwells in secret; and then thy Father, who sees what is done in secret, will reward thee.

READING III   Leg. Major, chap. V, 6-8
A Reading from the Major Life by St. Bonaventure

He was anxious to see the friars observe the silence which is recommended in the Gospel, being careful at all times to avoid every thoughtless word for which they might be brought to account on the day of judgment (cf. Mt 12, 36): He used to be quite sharp in correcting any friar who indulged habitually in gossip, declaring that a prudent reserve helped to maintain purity of heart and was an important virtue. Sacred Scripture tells us, "Of life and death, tongue holds the keys" (Prv 18, 21), more because of its power of speech than because it can taste.

Francis did his utmost to encourage the friars to lead austere lives, but he had no time for exaggerated self-denial which excluded tender compassion or was not tempered with discretion. One night a friar who had fasted too long was tormented with hunger and could get no rest. Like a good shepherd, Francis realized how badly he was faring and called him. Then he put some bread before him and advised him gently to eat it, and began to eat himself first, to avoid embarrassing him. The friar overcame his embarrassment and began to eat; he was overjoyed at seeing the saint's exquisite tact which enabled him to relieve his material needs and gave him such a wonderful example. In the morning Francis called the whole community together and told them what had happened, taking the opportunity to tell them, "You should take an example from the charity involved, not from the fact that we indulged in food." He also taught them to practice prudence, not the prudence recommended by our fallen nature, but that practiced by Christ whose life is the model of all perfection.

In his present state of weakness man is incapable of imitating the crucified Lamb of God perfectly and avoiding all the stains of sin. And so Francis taught his friars by his own example that those who are trying to be perfect must cleanse themselves daily with tears of contrition. He had attained extraordinary purity of soul and body, yet he never ceased from purifying his spiritual vision with floods of tears and thought nothing of the fact that it was costing him his sight. As a result of his continual weeping, he developed serious eye-trouble, but when the doctor advised him to restrain his tears if he wanted to avoid losing his sight, he replied, "Brother doctor, we share this world's light in common with the flies; we must not refuse to enjoy the presence of everlasting light merely to save it. Our bodies were given the power of sight for the sake of our souls; the sight which our souls enjoy was not given us for the sake of our bodies." He preferred rather to lose his sight than to check the fervor of his spirit and restrain the tears which sharpened his spiritual vision and enabled him to see God. (*Omnibus,* pp. 667-668.)

23

AVAILABILITY
ALWAYS READY TO DO THE WILL OF THE LORD

1 Cor 9:19-27
A Reading from the First Letter of Paul to
the Corinthians

Thus nobody has any claim on me, and yet I have
made myself everybody's slave, to win more souls.
With the Jews I lived like a Jew, to win the Jews:
with those who keep the law, as one who keeps the
law (though the law had no claim on me), to win those
who kept the law; with those who are free of the law,
like one free of the law (not that I disowned all divine
law, but it was the law of Christ that bound me), to
win those who were free of the law. With the scrupulous, I behaved myself like one who is scrupulous, to
win the scrupulous. I have been everything by turns
to everybody, to bring everybody salvation.

All that I do, I do for the sake of the gospel prom-
ises, to win myself a share in them. You know well
enough that when men run in a race, the race is for
all, but the prize for one; run, then, for victory. Every
athlete must keep all his appetites under control; and
he does it to win a crown that fades, whereas ours is
imperishable. So I do not run my course like a man in
doubt of his goal; I do not fight my battle like a man

who wastes his blows on the air. I buffet my own body, and make it my slave; or I, who have preached to others, may myself be rejected as worthless.

READING II   Lk 12:35-44
A Reading from the Holy Gospel according to Luke

Your loins must be girt, and your lamps burning, and you yourselves like men awaiting their master's return from a wedding feast, so that they may open to him at once when he comes and knocks at the door. Blessed are those servants, whom their master will find watching when he comes; I promise you, he will gird himself, and make them sit down to meat, and minister to them. Whether he comes in the second quarter of the night or in the third, blessed are those servants if he finds them alert. Be sure of this; if the master of the house had known at what time the thief was coming, he would have kept watch, and not allowed his house to be broken open. You too, then, must stand ready; the Son of Man will come at an hour when you are not expecting him.

Hereupon Peter said to him, Lord, dost thou address this parable to us, or to all men? And the Lord answered, Who, then, is a faithful and wise steward, one whom his master will entrust with the care of the household, to give them their allowance of food at the appointed time? Blessed is that servant who is found doing this when his lord comes; I promise you, he will give him charge of all his goods.

READING III   Cel. I, nos. 29, 91
A Reading from the First Life
by Fr. Thomas of Celano

At this same time also, when another good man had
entered their religion, their number rose to eight.
Then the blessed Francis called them all together,
and telling them many things concerning the kingdom of God, the contempt of the world, the renunciation of their own will, and the subduing of their own
body, he separated them into four groups of two each
and said to them: "Go, my dearest brothers, two by
two into the various parts of the world, announcing to
men peace and repentance unto the forgiveness of sins,
and *be patient in tribulation,* confident that the Lord
will fulfill his purpose and his promise. To those who
put questions to you, reply humbly; bless those who
persecute you; give thanks to those who injure you
and calumniate you; because for these things there is
prepared for you an eternal kingdom." But they, ac-
cepting the command of holy obedience *with joy* and
great *gladness,* cast themselves upon the ground before St. Francis. But he embraced them and said to
each one with sweetness and affection: "Cast thy
thought upon the Lord, and he will nourish you." This
word he spoke whenever he transferred any brothers
in obedience. . . .

At a certain time the blessed and venerable father
Francis left behind the crowds of the world that were
coming together daily with the greatest devotion to
hear and see him, and he sought out a quiet and secret place of solitude, desiring to spend his time there

with God and to cleanse himself of any dust that may
have clung to him from his association with men. It
was his custom to divide up the time given him to
merit grace, and, as seemed necessary to him, to give
part of it to working for the good of his neighbors and
the rest to the blessed retirement of contemplation.
He therefore took with him just the very few companions to whom his holy life was better known than it
was to the rest, so that they might protect him from
the invasion and *disturbance of men* and respect and
preserve his quiet in all things. After he had remained there for a while and had acquired in an inex-
pressible way familiarity with God by his constant
prayer and frequent contemplation, he longed to
know what might be more acceptable to the eternal
King concerning himself or in himself or what might
happen. Most carefully he sought out and most pi-
ously longed to know in what manner, by what way,
and by what desire he might cling perfectly to the
Lord God according to his counsel and according to
the good pleasure of his will. This was always his
highest philosophy; this very great desire always
flamed in him while he lived, namely, to seek out
from the simple, from the wise, from the perfect and
imperfect, how he might attain the way of truth and
come to his highest good. (*Omnibus,* pp. 252 and 306).

24

DEVOTION

Rom 8:28-39
A Reading from the Letter of Paul to the Romans

Meanwhile, we are well assured that everything
helps to secure the good of those who love God, those
whom he has called in fulfilment of his design. All
those who from the first were known to him, he has
destined from the first to be moulded into the image of
his Son, who is thus to become the eldest-born among
many brethren. So predestined, he called them; so
called, he justified them; so justified, he glorified
them. When that is said, what follows? Who can be
our adversary, if God is on our side? He did not even
spare his own Son, but gave him up for us all; and
must not that gift be accompanied by the gift of all
else? Who will come forward to accuse God's elect,
when God acquits us? Who will pass sentence against
us, when Jesus Christ, who died, nay, has risen again,
and sits at the right hand of God, is pleading for us?
Who will separate us from the love of Christ? Will
affliction, or distress, or persecution, or hunger, or
nakedness, or peril, or the sword? For thy sake, says

the scripture, we face death at every moment, reckoned no better than sheep marked down for slaughter. Yet in all this we are conquerors, through him who has granted us his love. Of this I am fully persuaded; neither death nor life, no angels or principalities or powers, neither what is present nor what is to come, no force whatever, neither the height above us nor the depth beneath us, nor any other created thing, will be able to separate us from the love of God, which comes to us in Christ Jesus our Lord.

READING II   Mt 10:16-22, 26-33
A Reading from the Holy Gospel according to
Matthew

Remember, I am sending you out to be like sheep among wolves; you must be wary, then, as serpents, and yet innocent as doves. Do not put your trust in men; they will hand you over to courts of judgement, and scourge you in their synagogues; yes, and you will be brought before governors and kings on my account, so that you can bear witness before them, and before the Gentiles. Only, when they hand you over thus, do not consider anxiously what you are to say or how you are to say it; words will be given you when the time comes; it is not you who speak, it is the Spirit of your Father that speaks in you. Brothers will be given up to execution by their brothers, and children by their fathers; children will rise up against their parents and will compass their deaths, and you will be hated by all men because you bear my name; that man will be saved, who endures to the last.

Do not, then, be afraid of them. What is veiled will all be revealed, what is hidden will all be known; what I have said to you under cover of darkness, you are to utter in the light of day; what has been whispered in your ears, you are to proclaim on the housetops. And there is no need to fear those who kill the body, but have no means of killing the soul; fear him more, who has the power to ruin body and soul in hell. Are not sparrows sold two for a penny? And yet it is impossible for one of them to fall to the ground without your heavenly Father's will. And as for you, he takes every hair of your head into his reckoning. Do not be afraid, then; you count for more than a host of sparrows. And now, whoever acknowledges me before men, I too will acknowledge him before my Father who is in heaven; and whoever disowns me before men, before my Father in heaven I too will disown him.

READING III   Letter to All the Faithful
A Reading from the Writings of St. Francis

Then, as his passion drew near, he celebrated the Pasch with his disciples and, taking bread, he *blessed and broke, and gave to his disciples, and said, Take and eat; this is my body. And taking a cup, he gave thanks and gave it to them, saying, This is my blood of the new covenant, which is being shed for many unto*

the forgiveness of sins (Mt 26: 26-29). And he prayed
to his Father, too, saying, *Father, if it is possible, let
this cup pass away from me* (Mt 26: 39); and his sweat
fell to the ground like thick drops of blood (cf. Lk 22:
44). Yet he bowed to his Father's will and said,
*Father, thy will be done; yet not as I will, but as thou
willest* (Mt 26: 42 and 39). And it was the Father's will
that his blessed and glorious Son, whom he gave to us
and who was born for our sake, should offer himself
by his own blood as a sacrifice and victim on the altar
of the cross; and this, not for himself, through whom
all things were made (Jn 1: 3), but for our sins, *leaving
us an example that* we *may follow in his steps* (1 Pt 2:
21). It is the Father's will that we should all be saved
by the Son, and that we should receive him with a
pure heart and chaste body. But very few are anxious
to receive him, or want to be saved by him, although
his *yoke is easy, and* his *burden light* (Mt 11: 30).

All those who refuse to *taste and see how good the
Lord is* (Ps 33: 9) and who love *the darkness rather
than the light* (Jn 3: 19) are under a curse. It is God's
commandments they refuse to obey and so it is of
them the Prophet says, *You rebuke the accursed
proud who turn away from your commands* (Ps 118:
21). On the other hand, those who love God are happy
and blessed. They do as our Lord himself tells us in
the Gospel, *Thou shalt love the Lord thy God with thy
whole heart, and with thy whole soul, . . . and thy
neighbour as thyself* (Mt 22: 37-39). We must love
God, then, and adore him with a pure heart and mind,
because this is what he seeks above all else, as he tells
us, *True worshippers will worship the Father in spirit*

and in truth (Jn 4: 23). All *who worship him must worship him in spirit and in truth* (Jn 4: 24). We should praise him and pray to him day and night, saying, *Our Father, who art in heaven* (Mt 6: 9), because *we must always pray and not lose heart* (Lk 18:1)....

Besides this, we must *bring forth therefore fruits befitting repentance* (Lk 3: 8) and love our neighbours as ourselves. Anyone who will not or cannot love his neighbour as himself should at least do him good and not do him any harm.

Those who have been entrusted with the power of judging others should pass judgement mercifully, just as they themselves hope to obtain mercy from God. *For judgement is without mercy to him who has not shown mercy* (Jas 2: 13). We must be charitable, too, and humble, and give alms, because they wash the stains of sin from our souls. We lose everything which we leave behind us in this world; we can bring with us only the right to a reward for our charity and the alms we have given. For these we shall receive a reward, a just retribution from God.

We are also bound to fast and avoid vice and sin, taking care not to give way to excess in food and drink, and we must be Catholics. We should visit churches often and show great reverence for the clergy, not just for them personally, for they may be sinners, but because of their high office, for it is they who administer the most holy Body and Blood of our Lord Jesus Christ. They offer It in sacrifice at the altar, and it is they who receive It and administer It to others....

Our Lord says in the Gospel, It is from the heart of man that all vice and sin comes (cf. Mt 15: 18-19), and he tells us, *Love your enemies; do good to those who hate you* (Lk 6: 27). We are bound to order our lives according to the precepts and counsels of our Lord Jesus Christ, and so we must renounce self and bring our lower nature into subjection under the yoke of obedience; this is what we have all promised God. (*Omnibus,* pp. 93-95.)

25

THE GRACE OF WORKING

READING I   1 Cor 3:1-15
A Reading from the First Letter of Paul to the Corinthians

And when I preached to you, I had to approach you as men with natural, not with spiritual thoughts. You were little children in Christ's nursery, and I gave you milk, not meat; you were not strong enough for it. You are not strong enough for it even now; nature still lives in you. Do not these rivalries, these dissensions among you shew that nature is still alive, that you are guided by human standards? When one of you says, I am for Paul, and another, I am for Apollo, are not these human thoughts? Why, what is Apollo, what is Paul? Only the ministers of the God in whom your faith rests, who have brought that faith to each of you in the measure God granted. It was for me to plant the seed, for Apollo to water it, but it was God who gave the increase. And if so, the man who plants, the man who waters, count for nothing; God is everything, since it is he who gives the increase. This man plants, that man waters; it is all one. And yet either will receive his own wages, in proportion to his own work. You are a field of God's tilling, a structure of God's design; and we are only his assistants.

With what grace God has bestowed on me, I have laid a foundation as a careful architect should; it is left for someone else to build upon it. Only, whoever builds on it must be careful how he builds. The foundation which has been laid is the only one which anybody can lay; I mean Jesus Christ. But on this foundation different men will build in gold, silver, precious stones, wood, grass, or straw, and each man's workmanship will be plainly seen. It is the day of the Lord that will disclose it, since that day is to reveal itself in fire, and fire will test the quality of each man's workmanship. He will receive a reward, if the building he has added on stands firm; if it is burnt up, he will be the loser; and yet he himself will be saved, though only as men are saved by passing through fire.

READING II   Mt 20:1-16
A Reading from the Holy Gospel according to
Matthew

Here is an image of the kingdom of heaven; a rich man went out at day-break to hire labourers for work in his vineyard; and when he sent them out into his vineyard he agreed with the labourers on a silver piece for the day's wages. About the third hour he came out again, and found others standing idle in the market-place; and to these also he said, Away with you to the vineyard like the others; you shall have whatever payment is fair. Away they went; and at noon, and once more at the ninth hour, he came out and did the like. Yet he found others standing there when he came out at the eleventh hour; How is it, he said to them, that you are standing here, and have done nothing all the day? They told him, It is because nobody has hired us; and he said, Away with you to the vineyard like the rest.

And now it was evening, and the owner of the vineyard said to his bailiff, Send for the workmen and pay them their wages, beginning with the last comers and going back to the first. And so the men who were hired about the eleventh hour came forward, and each was paid a silver piece. So that when the others came, who were hired first, they hoped to receive more. But they were paid a silver piece each, like their fellows. And they were indignant with the rich man over their pay. Here are these late-comers, they said, who have worked but one hour, and thou hast made no difference between them and us, who have borne the day's burden and the heat. But he answered one of them thus; My friend, I am not doing thee a wrong; did we not agree on a silver piece for thy wages? Take what is thy due, and away with thee; it is my pleasure to give as much to this late-comer as thee. Am I not free to use my money as I will? Must thou give me sour looks, because I am generous? So it is that they shall be first who were last, and they shall be last who were first. Many are called, but few are chosen.

READING III   Expos., chap. V
A Reading from Fr. Hugh of Digne's
Exposition of the Rule

By the grace of working is meant that skill or fit-
ness which anyone has received as a free gift from
God. Hence in the earlier Rule it was stated: "Let
those brethren who know how to work, labor and
exercise themselves in the art they understand, provided it is not unbecoming nor contrary to the salvation of their souls." And a little later, we read: "Let
everyone keep steadfast to the art or trade in which
he is skilled, according to the direction of his
superior."

There are, of course, many kinds of occupations in
which the friars must be engaged according to the
grace given each one, such as the striving for knowledge, the practice of humility or piety or charity or
other virtues, the exercise of governing, or of providing, or of other services as may be assigned to various
ones. Outside the time set aside for Divine Office, it is
becoming that everyone who is able should be engaged in some occupation.

Those who have formerly been accustomed to work,
are most blameworthy if they refuse to work now—
unless they are engaged in something better. For
spiritual work—being more excellent—excuses from
bodily labor. For, as the Saint remarks: "In the same
proportion as the spirit is superior to the body, so
spiritual exercises are more fruitful than bodily en-
deavors." Finally, idleness is the cess-pool of all vices.
Inded, idleness has been the teacher of much wick-

edness. On the other hand, he is not an idle religious who is not involved—either in practice or in contemplation—in those excesses which the religious state certainly does not exact.

The correct manner of working the Saint describes in the words: "Let them labor faithfully and devoutly, so that, repelling idleness, the enemy of the soul, they do not extinguish the spirit of holy prayer and devotion, to which all temporal things must be subservient." This manner of working is fitting for the servants of God, so that neither faithfulness in the action, nor devotion of the will and of a good intention in the mind, nor discernment in the execution be lacking; so that it excludes idleness in such a manner that the spirit of devotion is not extinguished.

For a religious, no matter how involved he may be in external activities, must nevertheless always say his prayers with devotion. It is a serious fault to neglect God's work on account of worldly occupations or activities. A faithful and prudent servant knows how to serve the Lord, now in the role of Mary, now in the role of Martha, offering him various courses of service in accordance with the changing commands.

Under the pretext of this precaution, some worldly-minded try to justify their idleness, saying that the spirit of devotion is extinguished in them whenever their superiors impose any work on them. But the spirit of prayer and devotion is not extinguished, as long as they do not become so absorbed in their work that they are hindered from devoutly saying the prayers prescribed by the Rule.

26

PILGRIMS, NOT RESIDENTS

READING I   Heb 13:1-3, 5-18, 20-21
A Reading from the Letter of Paul to the Hebrews

Let brotherly love be firmly established among you;
and do not forget to shew hospitality; in doing this,
men have before now entertained angels unawares.
Remember those who are in prison, as if you were
prisoners too; those who endure suffering, since you
have mortal bodies of your own.

The love of money should not dwell in your
thoughts; be content with what you have. God himself
has told us, I will never forsake thee, never abandon
thee; so that we can say with confidence, The Lord is
my champion; I will not be afraid of what man can do
to me.

Do not forget those who have had charge of you, and
preached God's word to you; contemplate the happy
issue of the life they lived, and imitate their faith.
What Jesus Christ was yesterday, and is to-day, he
remains for ever. Do not be carried aside from your
course by a maze of new doctrines; what gives true
strength to a man's heart is gratitude, not obser-

vances in the matter of food, which never yet proved useful to those who followed them. We have an altar of our own, and it is not those who carry out the worship of the tabernacle that are qualified to eat its sacrifices. When the high priest takes the blood of beasts with him into the sanctuary, as an offering for sin, the bodies of those beasts have to be burned, away from the camp; and thus it was that Jesus, when he would sanctify the people through his own blood, suffered beyond the city gate. Let us, too, go out to him away from the camp, bearing the ignominy he bore; we have an everlasting city, but not here; our goal is the city that is one day to be. It is through him, then, that we must offer to God a continual sacrifice of praise, the tribute of lips that give thanks to his name. Meanwhile, you must remember to do good to others and give alms; God takes pleasure in such sacrifice as this.

Obey those who have charge of you, and yield to their will; they are keeping unwearied watch over your souls, because they know they will have an account to give. Make it a grateful task for them: it is your own loss if they find it a laborious effort. Pray for us; we trust we have a clear conscience, and the will to be honourable in all our dealings.

May God, the author of peace, who has raised our Lord Jesus Christ from the dead, that great shepherd, whose flock was bought with the blood of an eternal covenant, grant you every capacity for good, to do his will. May he carry out in you the design he sees best, through Jesus Christ, to whom glory belongs throughout all ages, Amen.

READING II   Lk 9:57-62
A Reading from the Holy Gospel according to Luke

As they went on their journey, a man said to him, I
will follow thee wherever thou art going. But Jesus
told him, Foxes have holes, and the birds of the air
their resting-places; the Son of Man has no-where to
lay his head. To another he said, Follow me, and he
answered, Lord, give me leave to go home and bury
my father first. But Jesus said to him, Leave the dead
to bury their dead; it is for thee to go out and proclaim
God's kingdom. And there was yet another who said,
Lord, I will follow thee, but first let me take leave of
my friends. To him Jesus said, No one who looks behind him, when he has once put his hand to the
plough, is fitted for the kingdom of God.

READING III   3 Soc., nos. 37-39
A Reading from the Life by the Three Companions

Some people listened gladly; but others only
mocked them as fools and humbugs, and refused them
admittance into their houses for fear they might be
thieves and make off with something. Thus in many
places they suffered innumerable trials and insults,
and, finding no hospitality, they were driven to take
shelter under the porticoes of the churches or houses.
    At that time two of them arrived in Florence, and in
begging through the city, they could find no house
ready to take them in. They came to one which had a

portico containing a baking oven, so they said to each other: "Here we might spend the night." They asked the mistress of the house whether, for love of God, she would give them hospitality. But when she refused to admit them into the house, they humbly begged to be allowed to sleep near the oven under the portico; but she was joined by her husband who, seeing the brothers in the portico, called and said: "Why did you allow those good-for-nothings to stay in the portico?" She replied that she had refused to let them into the house but had consented to their lying outside in the portico where there was nothing to steal but some wood. Her husband would not even allow her to lend the strangers any blankets in which to wrap themselves, though it was very cold; and this because he thought they were thieves and vagabonds. They spent a very frugal night near the oven, warmed only by the glow of divine love, and covered with the blankets of Lady Poverty; and then, very early, they went to the chief church for Matins.

After daybreak the mistress of the house went to the same church, and when she saw the brothers kneeling devoutly in prayer, she said to herself: "If these men had been vagabonds and scoundrels as my husband thought, they would not be praying with such reverence." She was still absorbed in these thoughts when a man named Guido began to give alms to all who were in the church, and when he came to the brothers he would also have given them money, but they refused. Then he said: "Why will you not accept money like the other poor?" Brother Bernard answered: "It is true we are poor, but to us poverty is

not the burden it is to others for we have become poor
voluntarily by the grace of God, and we wish to follow
his precepts." The man Guido then asked whether
they had ever possessed worldly goods; and from them
he learned that indeed they had been rich but had
sold everything and given all to the poor for love of
God. And he who answered thus was Brother Bernard, the first son of Saint Francis; and today we
believe him to have been indeed a saint, since on
earth he was the first to embrace peace and penitence
and to follow Francis by selling all he had and giving
it to the poor, according to the Gospel counsel of perfection. And he persevered to the end in holy poverty
and purity.

When the woman saw how the brothers refused
money, she went up to them saying that, if they were
willing, she would gladly receive them into her house
as guests for love of God. They answered humbly:
"God reward you for your good will." However, when
Guido heard that the brothers had found no lodging,
he took them home with him, saying: "This is the
lodging prepared for you by the Lord; stay here as
long as you will."

Giving thanks to God they stayed with him some
time, edifying him greatly by their words and example in the fear of the Lord so that he generously gave
many things to the poor. (*Omnibus,* pp. 926-928.)

27

PENANCE WITH JOY

READING I Col 1:24-29
A Reading from the Letter of Paul to the Colossians

Even as I write, I am glad of my sufferings on your behalf, as, in this mortal frame of mine, I help to pay off the debt which the afflictions of Christ still leave to be paid, for the sake of his body, the Church. When I entered its service I received a commission from God for the benefit of you Gentiles, to complete the preaching of his word among you. This was the secret that had been hidden from all the ages and generations of the past; now, he has revealed it to his saints, wishing to make known the manifold splendour of this secret among the Gentiles—Christ among you, your hope of glory. Him, then, we proclaim, warning every human being and instructing every human being as wisely as we may, so as to exhibit every human being perfect in Christ Jesus. It is for this that I labour, for this that I strive so anxiously; and with effect, so effectually does his power manifest itself in me.

READING II   Lk 17:5-10
A Reading from the Holy Gospel according to Luke

The apostles said to the Lord, Give us more faith.
And the Lord said, If you had faith, though it were
like a grain of mustard seed, you might say to this
mulberry tree, Uproot thyself and plant thyself in the
sea, and it would obey you.

If any one of you had a servant following the
plough, or herding the sheep, would he say to him,
when he came back from the farm. Go and fall to at
once? Would he not say to him, Prepare my supper,
and then gird thyself and wait upon me while I eat
and drink; thou shalt eat and drink thyself afterwards? Does he hold himself bound in gratitude to
such a servant, for obeying his commands? I do not
think it of him; and you, in the same way, when you
have done all that was commanded you, are to say,
We are servants, and worthless; it was our duty to do
what we have done.

READING III   Cel. I, no. 35; II, no. 128
A Reading from the Lives by Fr. Thomas of Celano

There was great rejoicing among them when they
saw and had nothing that might give them vain or
carnal pleasure. They began therefore to have in that
place commerce with holy poverty; and comforted ex-
ceedingly in the absence of all things that are of this
world, they resolved to cling to poverty everywhere

just as they were doing here. And because once they had put aside solicitude for earthly things, only the divine consolation gave them joy, they decreed and confirmed that they would not depart from its embraces no matter by what tribulations they might be shaken or by what temptations they might be led on. But, though the pleasantness of that place, which could contribute not a little toward a weakening of their true strength of mind, did not detain their affections, they nevertheless withdrew from it, lest a longer stay might entangle them even in some outward show of ownership; and, following their happy father, they went at that time to the Spoleto valley. They all conferred together, as true followers of justice, whether they should dwell among men or go to solitary places. But St. Francis, who did not trust in his own skill, but had recourse to holy prayer before all transactions, chose not to live for himself alone, but for him *who died for all,* knowing that he was sent for this that he might win for God the souls the devil was trying to snatch away....

Francis once saw a certain companion of his with a peevish and sad face, and not taking this lightly, he said to him: "It is not becoming for a servant of God to show himself sad or upset before men, but always he should show himself honorable. Examine your offenses in your room and weep and groan before your God. When you return to your brothers, put off your sorrow and conform yourself to the rest." And after a few more things he said: "They who are jealous of the salvation of men envy me greatly; they are always trying to disturb in my companions what they cannot disturb in me." So much, however, did he love a man who was full of spiritual joy that he had these words written down as an admonition to all at a certain general chapter: "Let the brothers beware lest they show themselves outwardly gloomy and sad hypocrites; but let them show themselves joyful in the Lord, cheerful and suitably gracious." (*Omnibus,* pp. 257-258 and 467-468.)

28

HERALDS OF THE GREAT KING

READING I   Col 1:12-23
A Reading from the Letter of Paul to the Colossians

Endure joyfully, thanking God our Father for making us fit to share the light which saints inherit, for rescuing us from the power of darkness, and transferring us to the kingdom of his beloved Son.

In the Son of God, in his blood, we find the redemption that sets us free from our sins. He is the true likeness of the God we cannot see; his is that first birth which precedes every act of creation. Yes, in him all created things took their being, heavenly and earthly, visible and invisible; what are thrones and dominions, what are princedoms and powers? They were all created through him and in him; he takes precedency of all, and in him all subsist. He too is that head whose body is the Church; it begins with him, since his was the first birth out of death; thus in every way the primacy was to become his. It was God's good pleasure to let all completeness dwell in him, and through him to win back all things, whether on earth or in heaven, into union with himself, making peace with them through his blood, shed on the cross. You, too, were once estranged from him; your minds were alienated from him by a life of sin; but now he has used Christ's natural body to win you back through his death, and so to bring you into his presence, holy, and spotless, and unreproved. But that means that you must be true to your faith, grounded in it, firmly established in it; nothing must shift you away from the hope you found in the gospel you once listened to. It is a gospel which has been preached to all creation under heaven, and I, Paul, have been brought into its service.

READING II   Jn 18:33-37
A Reading from the Holy Gospel according to John

So Pilate went back into the palace, and summoned Jesus; Art thou the king of the Jews? he asked. Dost thou say this of thy own accord, Jesus answered, or is it what others have told thee of me? And Pilate answered, Am I a Jew? It is thy own nation, and its chief priests, who have given thee up to me. What offence hast thou committed? My kingdom, said Jesus, does not belong to this world. If my kingdom were one which belonged to this world, my servants would be fighting, to prevent my falling into the hands of the Jews; but no, my kingdom does not take its origin here. Thou art a king, then? Pilate asked. And Jesus answered, It is thy own lips that have called me a king. What I was born for, what I came into the world for, is to bear witness of the truth. Whoever belongs to the truth, listens to my voice.

READING III   3 Soc., nos. 36-37
A Reading from the Life by the Three Companions

Saint Francis being already full of the grace of the Holy Spirit called the six brothers together in the wood surrounding Saint Mary of the Angels where they often gathered to pray; and there he foretold many future things. "Dear Brothers, let us consider our vocation, and how God, in his great mercy, called us not only for our salvation but for that of many; and to this end we are to go through the world exhorting all men and women by our example as well as by our words to do penance for their sins, and to live keeping in mind the commandments of God." And he added: "Do not be afraid to preach penance even though we appear ignorant and of no account. Put your trust in God who overcame the world; hope steadfastly in him who, by the Holy Spirit, speaks through you to exhort all to be converted to him and to observe his commandments. You will find some men to be faithful and kind and they will receive you gladly; but you will also find many who are unfaithful, proud, and blasphemous, and they will insult and injure you and your words. Therefore prepare your hearts to suffer everything humbly and patiently."

When the brothers heard these words they began to be afraid, but the saint said to them: "Do not fear; before long many noble and wise men will join us, kings and princes too, with numbers of men, and very many people will be converted to the Lord and he will multiply and increase this his family in the whole world."

After these words the saint blessed them; and thus
fortified, those godly men started out faithfully following Francis' directions. Whenever they came on a
wayside cross or church, they bowed in prayer, saying: "We adore you, O Lord Christ, and bless you in
all the churches in the world because by your holy
cross you have redeemed the world."

The people they met were extremely surprised because in dress and manner of life they were so different from all others, and appeared almost like wild
men of the woods. Whenever they came to a town or
village or castle or house, they spoke the words of
peace, comforting all, and exhorting men and women
to love and fear the Creator of heaven and earth, and
to observe his commands.

Many people asked where they came from, and to
what order they belonged; and though it was weari-
some to answer such numerous questions, they replied simply that they were penitents from Assisi;
and indeed their community was not yet organized as
a religious order. (*Omnibus,* pp. 925-926.)

29

THE EUCHARIST
I SEE NOTHING CORPOREALLY ...

READING I 1 Cor 10:16-17, 11:23-16
A Reading from the First Letter of Paul to
the Corinthians

Is not this cup we bless a participation in Christ's
blood? Is not the bread we break a participation in
Christ's body? The one bread makes us one body,
though we are many in number; the same bread is
shared by all.

The tradition which I received from the Lord, and
handed on to you, is that the Lord Jesus, on the night
when he was being betrayed, took bread, and gave
thanks, and broke it, and said, Take, eat; this is my
body, given up for you. Do this for a commemoration
of me. And so with the cup, when supper was ended,
This cup, he said, is the new testament, in my blood.
Do this, whenever you drink it, for a commemoration
of me. So it is the Lord's death that you are heralding,
whenever you eat this bread and drink this cup, until
he comes.

READING II   Jn 6:48-58
A Reading from the Holy Gospel according to John

It is I who am the bread of life. Your fathers, who
ate manna in the desert, died none the less; the bread
which comes down from heaven is such that he who
eats of it never dies. I myself am the living bread that
has come down from heaven. If anyone eats of this
bread, he shall live for ever. And now, what is this
bread which I am to give? It is my flesh, given for the
life of the world.

Then the Jews fell to disputing with one another,
How can this man give us his flesh to eat? Whereupon
Jesus said to them, Believe me when I tell you this;
you can have no life in yourselves, unless you eat the
flesh of the Son of Man, and drink his blood. The man
who eats my flesh and drinks my blood enjoys eternal
life, and I will raise him up at the last day. My flesh is
real food, my blood is real drink. He who eats my
flesh, and drinks my blood, lives continually in me,
and I in him. As I live because of the Father, the
living Father who has sent me, so he who eats me will
live, in his turn, because of me.

READING III   Admonition I
A Reading from the Writings of St. Francis

Our Lord Jesus told his disciples, *I am the way, and
the truth, and the life. No one comes to the Father but
through me. If you had known me, you would also*

*have known my Father. And henceforth you do know
him, and you have seen him. Philip said to him, Lord,
show us the Father and it is enough for us. Jesus said
to him, Have I been so long a time with you, and you
have not known me? Philip, he who sees me sees also
the Father* (Jn 13: 6-9).

Sacred Scripture tells us that the Father dwells in
light inaccessible (1 Tim 6: 16) and that *God is spirit*
(Jn 4:24), and St. John adds, *No one at any time has
seen God* (Jn 1: 18). Because God is a spirit he can be
seen only in spirit; *It is the spirit that gives life; the
flesh profits nothing* (Jn 6: 64). But God the Son is
equal to the Father and so he too can be seen only in
the same way as the Father and the Holy Spirit. That
is why all those were condemned who saw our Lord
Jesus Christ in his humanity but did not see or believe in spirit in his divinity, that he was the true Son
of God. In the same way now, all those are damned
who see the sacrament of the Body of Christ which is
consecrated on the altar in the form of bread and wine
by the words of our Lord in the hands of the priest,
and do not see or believe in spirit and in God that this
is really the most holy Body and Blood of our Lord
Jesus Christ. It is the Most High himself who has told
us, This is my Body and Blood *of the new covenant*
(Mk 14: 22-24), and, *He who eats my flesh and drinks
my blood has life everlasting* (Jn 6: 55).

And so it is really the Spirit of God who dwells in
his faithful who receive the most holy Body and Blood
of our Lord. Anyone who does not have this Spirit and
presumes to receive him *eats and drinks judgement to
himself* (1 Cor 11: 29). And so we may ask in the

words of Scripture, *Men of rank, how long will you be dull of hèart?* (Ps 4: 3). Why do you refuse to recognize the truth *and believe in the Son of God?* (Jn 9: 35) Every day he humbles himself just as he did when he came from his *heavenly throne* (Wis 18: 15) into the Virgin's womb; every day he comes to us and lets us see him in abjection, when he descends from the bosom of the Father into the hands of the priest at the altar. He shows himself to us in this sacred bread just as he once appeared to his apostles in real flesh. With their own eyes they saw only his flesh, but they believed that he was God, because they contemplated him with the eyes of the spirit. We, too, with our own eyes, see only bread and wine, but we must see further and firmly believe that this is his most holy Body and Blood, living and true. In this way our Lord remains continually with his followers, as he promised, *Behold, I am with you all days, even unto the consummation of the world* (Mt 28: 20). (*Omnibus,* pp. 77-79.)

30

DEVOTION TO
THE BLESSED VIRGIN MARY

READING I   Prv 8:22-31
A Reading from the Book of Proverbs

Not yet had he made the earth, or the rivers, or the solid framework of the world. I was there when he built the heavens, when he fenced in the waters with a vault inviolable, when he fixed the sky overhead, and levelled the fountain-springs of the deep. I was there when he enclosed the sea within its confines, forbidding the waters to transgress their assigned limits, when he poised the foundations of the world. I was at his side, a master-workman, my delight increasing with each day, as I made play before him all the while; made play in this world of dust, with the sons of Adam for my playfellows.

READING II   Lk 1: 26-38
A Reading from the Holy Gospel according to Luke

When the sixth month came, God sent the angel
Gabriel to a city of Galilee called Nazareth, where a
virgin dwelt, betrothed to a man of David's lineage;
his name was Joseph, and the virgin's name was
Mary. Into her presence the angel came, and said,
Hail, thou who art full of grace; the Lord is with thee;
blessed art thou among women. She was much
perplexed at hearing him speak so, and cast about in
her mind, what she was to make of such a greeting.
Then the angel said to her, Mary, do not be afraid;
thou hast found favour in the sight of God. And behold, thou shalt conceive in thy womb, and shalt bear
a son, and shalt call him Jesus. He shall be great, and
men will know him for the Son of the most High; the
Lord God will give him the throne of his father David,
and he shall reign over the house of Jacob eternally;
his kingdom shall never have an end. But Mary said
to the angel, How can that be, since I have no knowledge of man? And the angel answered her, The Holy
Spirit will come upon thee, and the power of the most
High will overshadow thee. Thus this holy offspring
of thine shall be known for the Son of God. See, moreover, how it fares with thy cousin Elizabeth; she is
old, yet she too has conceived a son; she who was
reproached with barrenness is now in her sixth
month, to prove that nothing can be impossible with
God. And Mary said, Behold the handmaid of the
Lord; let it be unto me according to thy word. And
with that the angel left her.

READING III   Leg Major, chaps. II, 8; III, 1; IX, 3
A Reading from the Major Life by St. Bonaventure

When he had finished there, he came to a place called the Portiuncula where there was an old church dedicated to the Virgin Mother of God which was now abandoned with no one to look after it. Francis had great devotion to the Queen of the world and when he saw that the church was deserted, he began to live there constantly in order to repair it. He heard that the angels often visited it, so that it used to be called St. Mary of the Angels, and he decided to stay there permanently out of reverence for the angels and love for the Mother of Christ. He loved this spot more than any other in the world. It was here that he began his religious life in a very small way; it was here that he made such extraordinary progress, and it was here that he came to a happy end. When he was dying, he commended this spot above all others to the friars, because it was most dear to the Blessed Virgin.

Before entering the Order, one of the friars had a vision about the Portiuncula. He saw a huge crowd of blind folk kneeling in a circle about the church and looking up to heaven. With tearful voices and out-stretched hands, they cried out to God, begging him to have pity on them and give them sight. Then a brilliant light descended from heaven and enveloped them all, giving them back their sight and the health they longed for.

This was the place where St. Francis founded the Order of Friars Minor by divine inspiration and it was Divine Providence which led him to repair three churches before he founded the Order and began to preach the Gospel. This meant that he progressed from material things to more spiritual achievements, from lesser to greater, in due order, and it gave a prophetic indication of what he would accomplish later. Like the three buildings he repaired, Christ's church was to be renewed in three different ways under Francis' guidance and according to his Rule and teaching, and the three-fold army of those who are to be saved was to win victory. We can now see that this prophecy has come true. . . .

As he was living there by the church of our Lady, Francis prayed to her who had conceived the Word, full of grace and truth, begging her insistently and with tears to become his Advocate. Then he was granted the true spirit of the Gospel by the intercession of the Mother of Mercy and he brought it to fruition. . . .

He embraced the Mother of our Lord Jesus with indescribable love because, as he said, it was she who made the Lord of majesty our brother, and through her we found mercy. After Christ, he put all his trust in her and took her as his patroness for himself and his friars. In her honor he fasted every year from the feast of Saints Peter and Paul until the Assumption. (*Omnibus,* pp. 645-646 and 699.)

31

MEEK, PEACEFUL, MODEST

READING I   1 Cor 1:26-31
A Reading from the First Letter of Paul to the
Corinthians

Consider, brethren, the circumstances of your own
calling; not many of you are wise, in the world's fashion, not many powerful, not many well born. No, God
has chosen what the world holds foolish, so as to
abash the wise, God has chosen what the world holds
weak, so as to abash the strong. God has chosen what
the world holds base and contemptible, nay, has chosen what is nothing, so as to bring to nothing what is
now in being; no human creature was to have any
ground for boasting, in the presence of God. It is from
him that you take your origin, through Christ Jesus,
whom God gave us to be all our wisdom, our justifica-
tion, our santification, and our atonement; so that the
scripture might be fulfilled, If anyone boasts, let him
make his boast in the Lord.

READING II   Lk 12:32-34
A Reading from the Holy Gospel according to Luke

Do not be afraid, you, my little flock. Your Father
has determined to give you his kingdom. Sell what
you have, and give alms, so providing yourselves with
a purse that time cannot wear holes in, an inexhaust-
ible treasure laid up in heaven, where no thief comes
near, no moth consumes. Where your treasure-house
is, there your heart is too.

READING III   Expos., chap. III
A Reading from Fr. Hugh of Digne's
Exposition of the Rule

We read that Blessed Francis, imitating the example of our Savior, sent his friars out into the world in
groups of two. Even to-day he gives his directions to
the thousands who go out into the world, recommend-
ing to them the solace of mutual company and integ-
rity and approving a means of avoiding quarrels
which could arise between them.

"Let them not dispute among themselves," he says,
"nor contend in words." This admonition has refer-
ence to the friars themselves, as is evident from the
following words when he says: "Let them not judge
others," that is, outsiders. It is neither becoming nor
profitable for the friars to go about singly. Woe to the
man who travels alone; for if he should fall, he has no
one to help him rise again. Quarreling is never be-

coming among brothers or companions, but one must cautiously put up with a fellow-traveler, even if he shows himself to be an annoyance. To quarrel with one's companion is the vilest kind of behavior. A prudent person is ashamed to start a quarrel, even when he is insulted.

"Let them not dispute among themselves," the Saint says, "nor contend in words; but let them be meek, peaceful, modest, gentle and humble, speaking courteously to everyone, as is becoming." At this point, the Saint—according to the norm of the Gospel—excellently teaches how the friars who appear as a light to the Gentiles, must let their light shine before men, and how those who act otherwise seriously impair the good example of their lives.

For as the friars by their harmony among themselves and towards others, by their moderation in eating and drinking, by their meekness and humility in manners, and by their edifying and devout conversation, prove themselves as God's ministers and teachers of the Gospel, so by their quarrels and dissensions, by their gluttony and drunkenness, by their fastidious eating of rich foods and other delicacies— such as are unbecoming even for people out in the world—they make themselves abominable as men striving after perfection. All worldly manners or conversations and all undisciplined expressions only vilify and confound.

"Speaking courteously to everyone," he says, "as is becoming." For courteous speech among men—who pay closest attention to this—is not befitting the friars, so that foolish talking or scurrility should not even be named among them, as becomes saints. But let all their speech be always in thanksgiving and seasoned with salt. For they are the salt of the earth to serve as a seasoning for men; they are sent like the servants in the Gospel to invite men to the banquet. But if salt loses its flavor, wherewith shall it be salted?

It is extremely shameful for a preacher of the Gospel to have recourse to worldly fables. The very sacredness of the Word rules out all worldly pompousness, harshness, or any other worldly method. In this sense the Rule requires us to speak courteously not only to prominent persons, but to all—even household servants and persons of lowly rank. It is not fitting for a religious person to speak in the tongue of the world.